CELEBRATION OF HAND-HOOKED RUGS 28

2018 Edition

Editor
Debra Smith

Coordinator
Jessica Thelander

Designer
Brittnee Heller

Customer Service
Ampry Publishing, LLC
rughook@amprycp.com

Publisher
Ampry Publishing, LLC

Rug photographs provided by the artists unless otherwise noted.

Rug Hooking (ISSN 1045-4373) is published five times a year in Jan./Feb., March/April/May, June/July/Aug., Sept./Oct., and Nov./Dec. by Ampry Publishing, LLC, 3400 Dundee Road, Suite 220, Northbrook, IL 60062.
A publication of

HOOKING

P.O. Box 388
Shermans Dale, PA 17090

www.rughookingmagazine.com
rughook@amprycp.com

ISBN: 978-1-945550-32-4
Printed in U.S.A.

WELCOME TO
What's New?

The title of our annual publication, *Celebration of Hand-Hooked Rugs*, is doubly appropriate this year as we celebrate the thirtieth birthday of our flagship publication, **Rug Hooking** magazine. And we can't think of any better birthday gift than sharing the creativity and talent apparent in the magnificent rugs displayed in this year's book. From touching tributes to loved ones to stately floral pieces to wacky and delightful vignettes, *Celebration 28* is a snapshot of the accomplishments of the rug hooking community.

As we were approaching **Rug Hooking** magazine's big milestone, we asked ourselves what we could do to get Celebration in on the fun, and we came up with some exciting ideas.

To start, for the first time in *Celebration's* history, we awarded prizes to our three highest scoring rugs. We're thrilled for our first place entry, *The Fish Carpet,* by Peggy Peacock; our second place entry, *Tiger Close Up,* by Judy Carter; and our third place entry, *Honest Eds,* by Trish Johnson. All three show the incredible skill and artistry in the community, and we hope they'll inspire future generations of rug hookers.

In addition to awarding prizes, we've launched our very own Celebration Hall of Fame. We wanted to honor the rug hookers who had been featured in at least five editions of the book. We created galleries for each rug hooker, showcasing their works that have been featured in *Celebration* over the years, along with their reflections on their pieces and their journeys in the world of rug hooking. It wasn't easy! There were many rug hookers we hadn't heard from in a while, and there were even images that only existed as slides that needed to be digitized! In the end, we put together a beautiful gallery that celebrates the accomplishments of the rug hookers you've gotten to know year after year and allows you to appreciate the history of their work. You can check out the Hall of Fame at www.rughookingmagazine.com/Celebration-Hall-of-Fame. And who knows! Maybe someday, you too will join them!

While these new birthday developments are certainly exciting, we're as eager as ever to share with you the rugs presented in this year's *Celebration.* As you peruse the pages, we hope you'll find inspiration to help you celebrate with **Rug Hooking** all year long.

Jessica Thelander
Celebration Coordinator

Debra Smith
Rug Hooking Magazine Editor

ON THE COVER: *Ala Moana Memorial Lanterns,* designed and hooked by Barbara Prentice, 2017. See page 10 for the story of this stunning rug.

Table of Contents

RUGS BASED ON COMMERCIAL DESIGNS

RUGS BASED ON ADAPTATIONS

RUGS BASED ON PRIMITIVE DESIGNS

HONORABLE MENTIONS

Meet the Judges

With nearly 200 entries to evaluate, each containing four images, and judged on three criteria, these judges commit to spending hours upon hours of time deliberating on the outstanding works from the rug-hooking community. This is, of course, in addition to their other responsibilities with their work lives, home lives, social lives, and rug-hooking lives. We're so grateful to our thoughtful panel of judges for their time and consideration to help bring another edition of *Celebration* to life.

Anne Boissinot

Anne is a McGown-certified teacher who studied art at Sheridan College and resides in Canada. She taught rug hooking and the dyeing of materials for 45 years throughout Canada and the United States and has had the good fortune to have joined TIGHR and various groups in the rug-hooking world.

Anne has had the opportunity to travel by teaching and studying a variety of rug-hooking techniques from other countries, including Mexico. She's also been published in a variety of rug-hooking books and magazines in both Canada and the United States. This is her second time as a juror for *Celebration*, and she was thrilled to see the variety of pieces entered and the explosion of color, fibers, and design creativity that today's participants bring to the table.

Susan L. Feller

Susan was introduced to rug hooking in 1994. Historical traditions and the artistry of working with fibers in design drew her interest. The journey evolved into a pattern-making line, Ruckman Mill Farm, which continues under Green Mountain Hooked Rugs; vending nationally and curating rug hooking exhibits; networking and representing members on boards for ATHA, TIGHR, and the editorial board of *Rug Hooking* magazine; teaching design; and now practicing as a studio artist and earning awards in national juried exhibitions.

She is the author of *Design Basics for Rug Hookers* and *Design in a Box: Frakturs*. Susan received a fellowship from the Tamarack Foundation for the Arts to research and publish the textile work of West Virginians Blanche and Otha McDonald. This material is found at ArtWools.com/McDonalds and was featured in the Jan/Feb 2017 issue of *Rug Hooking* magazine.

Susan values the relationships developed through mutual interest in rug making and looks forward to developing new ones online and, especially, in person. You can find out more about her work at ArtWools.com.

Fritz Mitnick

Fritz Mitnick has been doing needlework for decades and hooking rugs since 1997. After deciding that rug hooking is the ultimate fiber art for her, she quit her job after 28 years as a youth services librarian to have more time to hook. An accredited McGown rug hooking teacher, she teaches in her home, at Pittsburgh area community and art centers, and at rug-hooking workshops and camps.

Her rugs and articles have appeared in *Rug Hooking* magazine, the *Wool Street Journal*, *ATHA News*, and the *McGown Guild Quarterly*. Fritz's *Pittsburgh Nocturne* was a *Celebration XV* honorable mention rug and the cover of the Jan/Feb 2008 issue of *Rug Hooking* magazine. Her rug *Look Out*, depicting a crow in the moonlight, was selected for *Celebration XVII*. *Mighty Moose* was a finalist in *Celebration XXI* in 2011, *Blackbird* was a finalist in *Celebration XXIII* in 2013, and *Quilt Sampler for Wide Cut* was a finalist in *Celebration 26* in 2016.

Some of Fritz's patterns are available through Honey Bee Hive (rughook.com). She is the past Region 6 representative for the Association of Traditional Hooking Artists, a member and former president of the Southern McGown Teachers Workshop, and a member of TIGHR, an international rug hooking organization.

Loretta Scena

Loretta is a McGown-certified traditional rug hooking teacher living on Long Island, New York. She is a member of ATHA, TIGHR, and the McGown National Guild. She is the current president of The Long Island Guild of Rugcrafting Artists, an organization that has reproduced several of the rugs that are featured in the houses in the Old Bethpage Village Restoration in Bethpage, New York.

Loretta teaches classes in her home studio as well as at guilds and rug camps in the United States. Her work has been featured in *Rug Hooking* magazine and the McGown newsletter.

Aaron

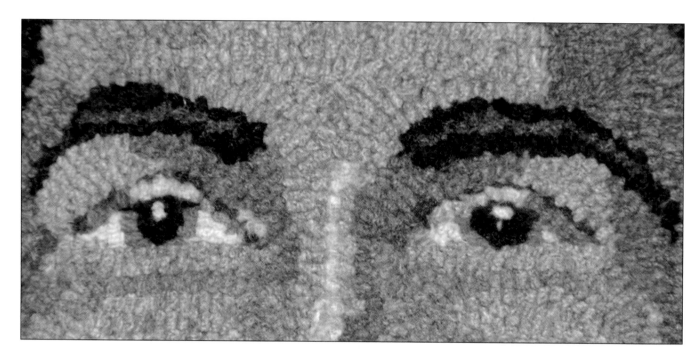

Our family lost Aaron just before Christmas in 2010 due to a seizure. After completing a memorial rug of Aaron's life a few years later, I still felt empty from his passing, and my grief was not subsiding. Looking for another way to help me in the healing process, I came across a black-and-white photograph of Aaron. I knew in my heart I had found what I needed to fill that void: to hook a portrait of him as lifelike as possible.

I remember seeing a rug a few years ago in *Rug Hooking* magazine that showed a lady hooked in color and her husband hooked in a grayscale to signify her loss. That rug stuck with me. When I got to the point where I could again hook a rug of Aaron, the grayscale monochrome was the way I felt I could show our family's loss. I was told that a monochrome was the most difficult way of hooking a rug. That became the challenge for me. I almost always use recycled wool, so I started collecting as many different grays as I could find.

My favorite section of the rug is the eyes. If the eyes are wrong, nothing else will be right. I believe that I captured my son's soul in his eyes. The most challenging section was Aaron's turtleneck. The portrait that I was working from was in black and white, so the turtleneck blended into his face. Nothing seemed to work until I thought of a film negative where everything is reversed: white is black, and black is white. So I changed the turtleneck to a darker color, and Aaron's face seemed to jump off the linen.

I didn't finish the rug in a traditional sense. The rug was stretched over a piece of Masonite that had been covered with linen to protect the back of the rug. Then the rug was placed in an antique frame used by Aaron's grandfather, Claude Harta. This rug taught me that portraits take a lot of commitment, especially when hooking a portrait of a child that you have lost. It is a very emotional ride, with ups and downs, as you relive that journey.

Russ Nichols
Green Valley, Arizona

Russ is currently retired but previously worked in the parks and recreation profession; he was also a professional photographer. He's enjoyed a number of crafts over the years, including pine needle basketry, pottery, quilting, embroidery, and cross stitch. He also does woodworking and is renovating a vintage 1961 Avion travel trailer. This is his first appearance in Celebration.

Aaron, 16" x 20", #3- and 4-cut recycled wool on linen. Designed and hooked by Russell L. Nichols, Green Valley, Arizona, 2016.

Ala Moana Memorial Lanterns

The Memorial lanterns are a custom of Japan, particularly the southern regions of the country, where they are lit during Obon festivals and other solemn occasions to pay tribute to the dead. Often people write prayers and poems to their lost loved ones in kanji, a Japanese system of writing using characters borrowed or adapted from Chinese writing. This tradition was brought to the islands of Hawai'i, where fleets of lanterns are launched from the South and North Shores on both American and Japanese holidays. I have lived in both Japan and Hawai'i and have merged many pictures together to design my own depiction of this occasion.

I drew my first pattern several years ago but was not satisfied with the design and set it aside. I redrew it after rethinking the pattern; I also asked Gail Dufresne to help me with the dip dyes for the water. I took a workshop at Hooked in the Mountains with Janet O'Connor, who taught how to turn your photographs into a rug. I put the original design away for a few years as it was lacking a focal point. I used first my own photos as a starting point and then moved the boxes and figures around like paper dolls. When I saw the canoe lantern, I knew I had a focal point. I intentionally cut off the front of the lanterns to make the image look like a Japanese woodblock print, which I love after seeing so many during my years in Japan.

I decided to go from a #8 cut in the foreground to a #3 cut in the background to achieve a sense of distance. The lanterns worked, but the water did not have the smooth look I wanted. The spots in my original wool made the waters of the South Shore of O'ahu look too turbulent. I had to pull it all out and re-dye some swatches instead. I used some shibori-dyed wool from Gail and some dyed silk in the water to make the reflections glow. The far edge of the water, which fades into an indistinct haze, was a challenge that my teacher, Roslyn Logsdon, helped me through. I hooked the far hills in a combination of wool, velvet, and novelty fabric, with halogen circles to depict the houses in the distance.

I did not want to bind the rug as I felt it would "stop" the picture, and I wanted it to flow outwards. My husband made a stretcher bar for the picture. I sewed custom-dyed wool—yellow for the bottom and a medium blue for the rest—around the rug and then stretched it around the wood, finishing the back with grosgrain ribbon.

Barbara Prentice
Springfield, Virginia

Barbara was a book buyer and trailing wife with her Navy officer husband before she became a docent for the National Museum of American History. She also volunteers in the archaeology department at George Washington's Mount Vernon historical site. This is her second appearance in Celebration.

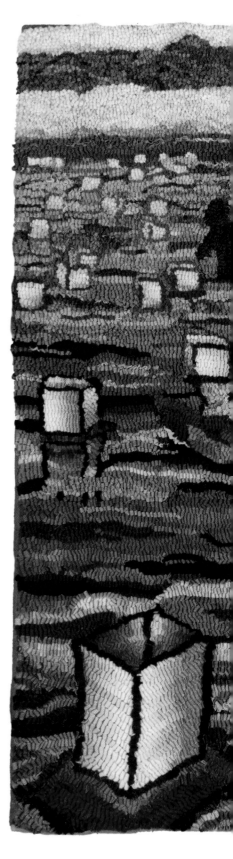

Ala Moana Memorial Lanterns, 36" x 30", #3- to 8-cut hand-dyed wool, silk, and novelty materials on linen. Designed and hooked by Barbara Prentice, Springfield, Virginia, 2017. BILL BISHOP

In The Judges' Eyes: *A limited palette that emphasizes the mood (solemn, special). Oh, then we see the silhouetted people actively participating. The finishing is professional and clean; Moving and visually stunning; Beautiful use of complementary colors, lovely finishing detail.*

America

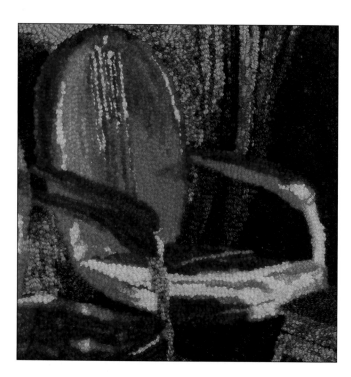

I went to visit my sister after taking part in the *Celebration 25* festivities at Sauder Village. At my bedside in her guest room was a book I created from photos I took of my grandparents' home in Illinois when I visited for my grandmother's funeral. I knew this would be my last time in the only home of theirs that I had ever known, so I wandered around taking photos of memories. That is what I consider this rug to be: a memory rug and the start of my family in America!

These chairs and other remnants of their garden sit in their garage, but the garage, built first, was where they had lived as they waited for the rest of their home to be built. The picture of these chairs—their chairs—sitting so silently in their garage grabbed my attention. I found the feelings of emptiness and melancholy haunting. This rug honors my grandparents and the dreams of all immigrants. They came from a troubled country with no money, not speaking a word of English. They worked hard, became citizens, built a home, and put a son through college. They loved to sit outdoors in these chairs at the end of a sultry Midwestern summer day and watch their grandchildren play.

My goal was to present what I saw in the picture as best as I could, paying particular attention to the clarity of the light and the brightness and focus of the chairs. There is a mottled quality to the blend of the colors in the original pictures, which I intensified in Photoshop® by using the film grain filter. I was excited by the unexpected boldness this gave to the image. To achieve this graphic boldness in my rug, I attempted spot dyeing for the first time. I did several tests, starting with the technique in Gene Shepherd's *Prepared to Dye*. I moved to the oven first, with the yarn in a flat pan, and then finally to the yarn wrapped in aluminum foil. The spots were best defined when I limited the amount of water used and cooked the yarn for about an hour. The dots were too big, however, for the gentle movement of the back wall. I had been regularly splitting the 3-ply yarn to create thinner yarn for smaller spaces. I kept all of the loose strands. I tried hooking these loose strands in with 2-ply versions of the yarn in a different color, and . . . Eureka! I was able to achieve the softer blend and smaller dots that I wanted. It's a new technique for me that I see being very useful in the future.

I work as a designer in the theater, which is a communal art, but I have also always pursued my own individual expression through drawing, watercolor, and knitting. Hooking hit the spot. When hooking with yarn, my subjects come alive in ways they had not before. It is a thrill!

In The Judges' Eyes: *Effective use of color, with warm subject and cool background evoking a comfortable place to visit. The materials and direction of each line add depth and definition. Back shows a consistency in punchwork that is evident on the front. This composition artistically renders a nostalgic feeling.*

Nancy Thun
Hoboken, New Jersey

Nancy has primarily worked on Broadway as an associate set designer, working with London-based designers for shows such as Mamma Mia, Jersey Boys, *and* Charlie and the Chocolate Factory. *This is her fourth appearance in* Celebration.

America, 30" x 41", hand-dyed wool yarn on cotton rug warp. Designed and hooked by Nancy Thun, Hoboken, New Jersey, 2017.

At Jesus' Feet

*A*t Jesus' Feet is an abstract piece as well as a geometric. Each block was created with the dark worms and red outline (sometimes one row, sometimes two) being the constant through the rug. I have a large collection of neutral textures, which I wanted to contrast with the vibrant red. The foot is hooked so that, up close, you do not see the foot of Jesus, but when you stand back and absorb first the background, then the object, you realize what the object is on the rug. It creates a moving moment. Red in the center of the rug easily could have become a bull's eye. That's why I broke the background up with squares outlined in red.

This rug did not start out as the foot of Jesus, but it evolved into that. Using textures mixed with dyed wool is what created the dimension and allowed the foot to take shape. I never use rug tape on my rugs. I roll the edges forward and whip them. This rug was a gift for my friend Jeannie Pilson, at the Caraway Baptist Camp and Conference Center in Ashboro, North Carolina. It was also displayed at the Sauder Village 2017 exhibit "Man Made."

After doing needlework for twenty-five years, I picked up an old rug-hooking book at a flea market and

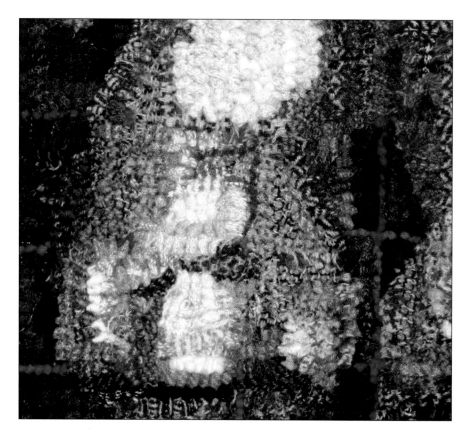

thought, "There's only one stitch here. I could do this." I was self-taught for two years until I found my home teacher, Jane Olson, who I studied with for many years. I got my McGown Teaching Certificate in 1997, the first man to be certified in the program.

I think the idea of choosing my own colors was the main draw for me. I have been involved in many aspects of the needle arts for over fifty years. I started with needlepoint at age fifteen and progressed from there. I have now been rug hooking for twenty-five years.

In The Judges' Eyes: *Dramatic palette evokes the mood of event. Interesting to carry the red into grid, adds depth; Unusual piece, a large, interesting approach to the subject; An unusual subject, well-hooked; Powerful piece. Nicely hooked.*

Eric Sandberg
Onancock, Virginia

Eric retired in 2000 from the film industry, where he was a motion picture costumer in Los Angeles for twenty-eight years, working with such notables as Steven Spielberg, Jack Nicholson, and Tom Hanks. For the next fifteen years, he was a circuit rug-hooking teacher, traveling all over the US and Canada, and served as the director of Caraway Rug School. This is his fourth appearance in Celebration.

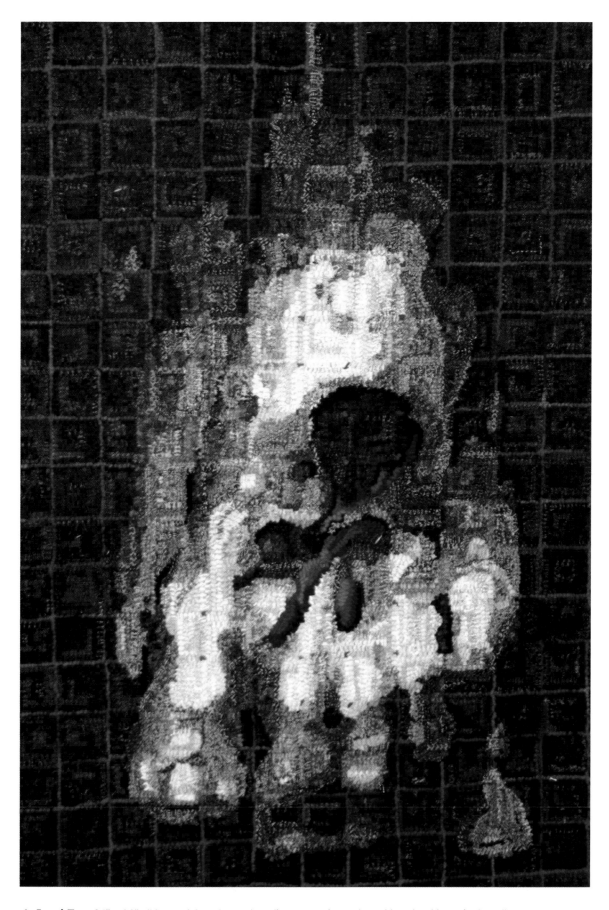

At Jesus' Feet, 26" x 38", #3- and 8-cut wool on linen. Designed and hooked by Eric Sandberg, Onancock, Virginia, 2016. LISANNE MILLER

Back Lit Jack Pine

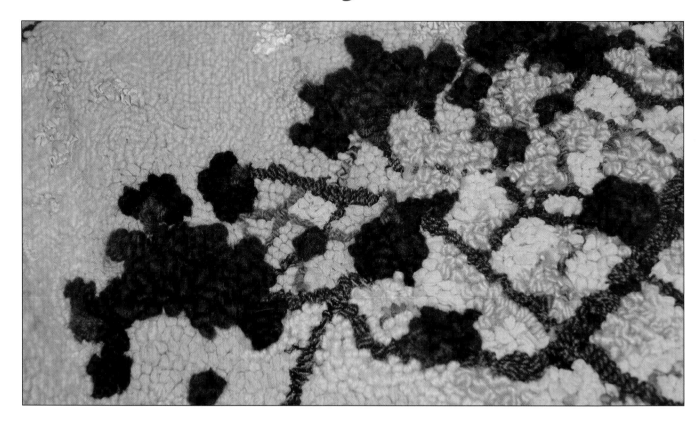

I was inspired to create this rug from seeing these big old jack pines on the west side of my yard. When the sun is low behind them, they are glorious. I used some silk, for its sheen, in the background to help give it a glow. I wanted to use a good variety of yellows and light greens to give the effect of light through the branches. For the tree trunks, I used a variety of overdyed wool tweeds to provide the rough texture.

The raised tree trunks proved to be a challenge. They were hooked separately and then attached. My first attempt at padding them resulted in too much puffing at the back. On the second try, I sewed one side down, cut a thin layer of batting, and tacked it in place. Then I added a thicker, narrower layer and attached the other side, being careful to thin out the batting as I went. At the top of the hanging, the trunk gradually merges into the work. I found the best way to do this was to overlap the trunk and background and hook through both. Since this piece, I have gone on to use more raised elements in my work.

Because of the weight, size, and shape of this work, I decided to use artist canvas when finishing the back. It had good weight, doesn't fray too badly, and could be cut to match the shape. I could then paint it to blend with the front.

I first started rug hooking when a dear aunt, who was then in her eighties, wanted help in starting one last rug. I jumped at the chance and told her I would help as long as she taught me how to hook! I enjoy rug hooking because I love the creativity of it, have a love affair with fabric and texture, and find the physical work something I can get totally lost in.

Donna Brunner
Westerose, Alberta, Canada

Donna is an artist who paints pots and has dabbled in jewelry making and weaving. Her work has been shown at the Alberta Craft Council, and she is a member of TIGHR. This is her first appearance in Celebration.

Back Lit Jack Pine, 47" x 30", hand-cut wool and silk on linen. Designed and hooked by Donna Brunner, Westerose, Alberta, Canada, 2016.

In The Judges' Eyes: *Every loop is working to evoke the moment. Tiny patches of light amongst medium values bring our attention to further depth. The finish, as my grandmother would say, declares the skill/artistry of the maker. Can't wait to see this in person; Harmonious use of a variety of fibers. Great choice of finished shape and application.*

Barn

As I helped a friend prepare for her daughter's wedding reception, to be held in an old barn, I was taken with the daylight that shone through the vertical boards. The angle and the bulk of the old timbers that supported the roof also fascinated me. I took a photo with my cell phone camera and saved it for later.

When I transferred the photo on to the rug foundation cloth, I wanted to capture the sense of comfort one feels when standing inside a darkened barn. If I could create the look of a stage setting, that would heighten the drama. I remembered the term "proscenium arch" from my reading about theater. By adding the dark brown proscenium arch around the vertical light-and-board back wall, I could suggest three-dimensionality, which is furthered by extending the floorboards toward the viewer. All of this might give the viewer the sense of being inside the barn.

My goal of creating as much three-dimensionality as possible led me to focus a great deal of attention on the chair. I tried very hard to make it stand on the barn stage floor in near-three-dimensional readiness for whoever might enter the scene.

I purchased silk yarn from Halcyon Yarn to represent daylight. Its shine was an essential quality that I could not achieve as satisfactorily with any other material. A neighbor who was reconfiguring the stalls in his barn supplied the wood for the frame, which seemed absolutely fitting.

Starting and ending each horizontal row of loops at the exact right foundation hole was challenging. A second challenge was trying to depict a sense of depth. To achieve this, I used narrow, hand-cut strips for the furthest points and #4-cut strips for areas that are closer.

To finish the rug, I serged the foundation cloth, leaving about one inch all the way around the scene. I stapled the foundation to the back of the wooden frame, with the wool rug face showing through the frame's opening. I then covered the entire back with an acid-free mounting board that is stapled to the back of the frame.

When I began this ambitious project, I knew my goals but I did not know whether or not I would succeed in achieving them. I might easily have labored on and off for well more than a year, only to have a large hooked flop. I thought about that possibility as I worked, but I learned—or re-learned—that one has to try.

Melinda Russell
Alderson, West Virginia

Melinda is a retired lawyer. She's had pieces in a juried show at the Pittsburgh Center for the Arts and in an exhibition of contemporary rugs held at the Farnsworth Art Museum. Barn *has been exhibited at the Tamarack Cultural Center and at the West Virginia Art Museum. This is her first appearance in* Celebration.

Barn, 47½" x 35 ¼", #4-cut wool strips and silk yarn on monk's cloth. Designed and hooked by Melinda Russell, Alderson, West Virginia, 2016.

Brainchild

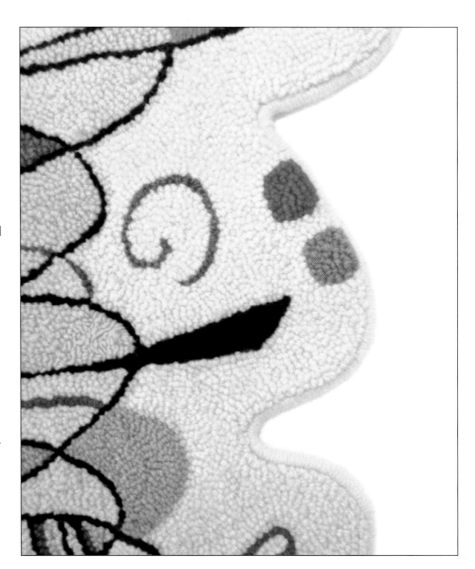

My subject matter started with the simple idea of a personal doodle I had drawn that caught my interest. I decided to enlarge the drawing, making it both oversized and dramatic, while maintaining the fun and interest of the original doodle. By choosing colors and patterns that complemented each other, I attempted to add visual interest to enhance the original sketch.

One of my main concerns was figuring out how to keep the integrity of the original doodle in this large format. I wanted to keep all the original flaws of the rug, so it still looks like a doodle and not a perfect rendition of one. That element is what I love most about my rug.

Getting the actual shape the way I wanted it was the most challenging aspect of this rug. I liked how all the lines and elements kept one's eye moving around the design in an interesting and pleasing manner. I liked the visual movement that was achieved and wanted to enhance this further by silhouetting the shape of my rug. I then finished my rug by cording it and whipstitching the edge.

I hooked my first rug in high school and included it in my art school portfolio. In 2007, I discovered the Craftsman's punch needle and started creating hand-hooked rugs, teaching myself all the techniques, including cording and whipstitching. I create all my own designs, which include subjects such as food, graphic images, patterns, and silhouetted shapes (all with a sense of humor).

In The Judges' Eyes: *It is the bold nipping in and out for the edging that makes this design. Choosing the whipped white nothingness takes our eye to the lines; Beautifully finished. Love the movement and energy.*

Wayne Bressler
New York, New York

Wayne has worked as an art director/graphic designer for various magazine publications in New York City for over twenty-five years. He enjoys illustrating and cartooning and has had six cartoons published in The New Yorker *magazine. This is his sixth appearance in* Celebration.

Brainchild, 39" x 67", wool rug yarn on monk's cloth. Designed and hooked by Wayne Bressler, New York, New York, 2017.

Celestial Spheres

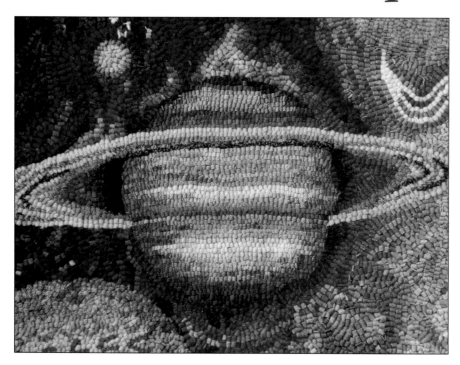

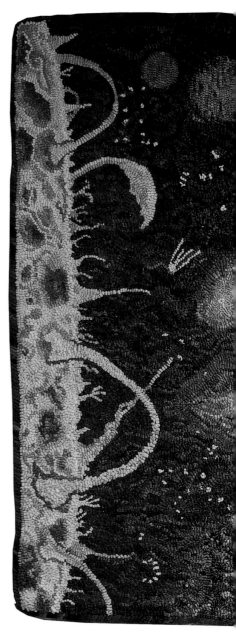

I consider *Celestial Spheres* to be an illustration of humankind's next frontier for becoming a multi-planet species. As a hooker who went to space camp for her fortieth birthday, I've been interested in anything and everything related to what's beyond Earth's atmosphere ever since I was a child watching the sky for Sputnik. Since then, I've devoured NASA's spectacular images of the solar system, Messier objects, and the Milky Way, courtesy of the Hubble and Spitzer telescopes and NASA's exploratory mission spacecraft. I've also followed SpaceX as it creates the necessary hardware and software to return the human race to above low Earth orbit (LEO)—the moon, Mars, and beyond.

When I signed up for Michele Micarelli's class at the Green Lake Hooking Camp in 2016, I decided to try to design and hook a large rug displaying some of the brightest and most striking NASA images, using some of Michele's advice and beautifully colored wool. The rug is primarily wool—as-is, overdyed, solids, and textures in cuts #3–8. To simulate some of the stars, I used metallic silver ribbon. I was also fortunate to find a blue wool with threads of metallic silver, which gives the rug some subtle sparkle.

I really wanted to use very vibrant colors for the spheres and other objects to provide good contrast against the blue-black-purple of space and within the objects themselves. Michele Micarelli dyed some of the brightest purples, pinks, blues, and oranges. All of the images attempt to replicate the colors of the objects shown in NASA photos, albeit some being false-colored photos that emphasize various features. Otherwise, the wool was from my stash or something that caught my eye at one of the hook-ins.

I love making a rug into a complex message by way of details. In this case, the rug not only displays the sun with spots and prominences, along with detailed images of the planets, but also some of their major moons; the Milky Way; some Messier objects; comets; the asteroid belt; the inferred Planet Nine; the dwarf planet, Pluto; and a selection of the major constellations. It's a snapshot of our current knowledge of what lies beyond our atmosphere.

Every part of a project is an adventure that requires imagination and creativity: coming up with a subject, creating a

Elaine Fischhoff
Lansing, Michigan

Elaine is a retired attorney. She's a member of ATHA Guild 132: the Wild Wooly Women. In addition to rug hooking, she's sewn some of her own clothes, along with knitting, crocheting, beading, flower pressing and displaying, watercolor, making twig furniture, and designing and embroidering rug labels. This is her first appearance in Celebration.

design, selecting colors of wool or other materials, deciding whether to include proddy or other techniques, adjusting the design and/or colors in the process of hooking as necessary to end up with a pleasing product—and finally enjoying the satisfaction of putting my rug on the floor and feeling very proud of the result.

In The Judges' Eyes: *All that warm energy in the solar system; Beautifully rich color and detail. Unique design very nicely put together; The small segment of the sun is fascinating. Hot stuff!*

Celestial Spheres, 65" x 40", #3- to 8-cut hand-dyed and as-is wool on linen. Designed and hooked by Elaine Fischhoff, Lansing, Michigan, 2017. ZIAD YOUSSFI

Deco Dress

This piece was inspired by a dress I used to own. This is the first of a series of dresses I plan to hook. I have always been attracted to different historical eras and like to imagine life during those times.

I chose to create this piece using pink and gray, which are historically accurate to the art deco period. I find that my rugs tell me what they want in terms of, for example, color and embellishments. I love to use gemstones on my hooked pieces, and this one told me it wanted lots of them! I also used some chiffon-type fabrics glued on top of dyed wool. I particularly love the fringes at the bottom of the dress. I can just imagine a flapper dancing and the fringes moving! I think because this is a unique piece, when it is in a show, people touch it a lot. One person doesn't make an impact, but after several hundred do it, it begins to look a little shop-worn. Please, when you see it in a show, do not touch!

The most challenging part of the dress was trying to keep everything even. It was a lot like hooking an Oriental—each side has to be exactly the same. I wasn't careful enough when drawing the pattern and had to redo parts of it. I added most of the gemstones before I started hooking and found I had to spend a lot of time repositioning them. I learned to be careful when drawing a geometric pattern. When you want both sides to match, draw one half, then flip the pattern over and draw the exact same thing on the other side.

I laid the finished piece on a piece of dyed wool and cut out around the dress, allowing a ¾" seam allowance. Then, with the right sides together, I folded in the seams and stitched around the edges. I then stitched in between my loops on the front of the dress. This allowed me to pull the backing right up to my hooking.

I first got started in rug hooking while I was on vacation and saw rug hooking in the back of a gift shop. I got a five-minute lesson, bought a pattern with precut strips, and have never looked back. I've tried lots of different crafts, from decorative finishing to stained glass. Rug hooking is the first craft that satisfies all of my creative urges. From creating a pattern to dyeing the wool to hooking a finished piece that is utterly unique, rug hooking is a gratifying form of expression.

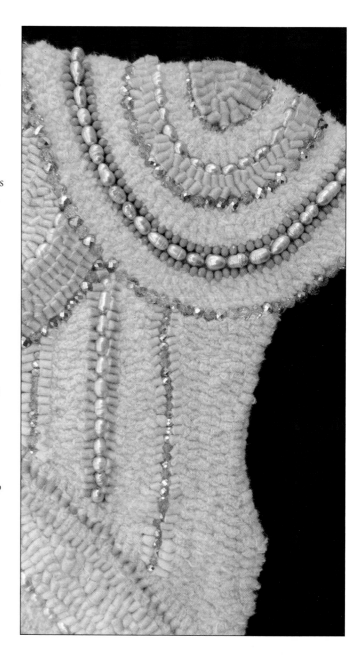

Cindy Irwin
Lancaster, Pennsylvania

Cindy likes to say she is a retired housewife and also teaches rug hooking. She is a member of ATHA, a board member of the National McGown Guild, and president of her local McGown guild. She's also a juried member of the Pennsylvania Guild of Crafters and assistant director of the Northern McGown Teachers Workshop. This is her eighth appearance in Celebration.

Deco Dress, 12" x 26", wool, polyester, pearls, crystals, and glass on monk's cloth. Inspired by a vintage dress and designed and hooked by Cindy Irwin, Lancaster, Pennsylvania, 2017.

Downhill

I live near Mt. Bachelor, Oregon, and I am fortunate enough to be able to ski an average of three times per week. I love the sport. I love the mountain. I love the cold on my face. I absolutely love the feeling I get when I fly down the mountain. And I love rug hooking. I love the feel of the wool in my hands. I love the feeling of accomplishment when I complete a rug. Combining the two loves only makes sense. After all, when you love what you do, everything else comes easy.

The Inuit language has many words for "snow." They describe sunlit sparkling snow, crusty snow, squeaky snow, and many more. They understand that how we see snow is an intricate combination of temperature, color, density, and distance observed. So how in the world do you put wool together for that? I studied many pictures of snow. I studied it every time I took a lift chair. I watched in the shade and in the sun. I took pictures of the distant mountains and the frozen sculptures it created in the trees. The snow was different in each setting.

There was so much snow to show: distant snow, flying snow, snow in the shadows. It was very apparent that I better understand hue and value. By using many colors and values, I was able to show depth, shadow, and distance. To create the depth in the close, flying snow, I simply made "bubbles of color" with my lightest values. I used blues, purples, pinks, greens, and yellows for this snow. Rarely did I use over a value of 1 in the close, flying. In fact, I got inventive and creative with values of 0 and -1. The distant snow is darker, yet still it has depth, so several colors of values 3 and 4 were used.

As everyone knows, snow glitters in the sunshine. I found some ribbon that had just the right amount of "snow crystals" and hooked in a stitch or two throughout the foreground. I wish the ribbon had

shown up better in the photographs, as it does sparkle like snow in the sun. Wool roving was used to create the billowing snow around the skier.

A big "thank you" needs to be said to those who helped me along the way. Thanks to Ingrid Hieronimus for her guidance and suggestions in getting the rug started in 2016. Thanks to Libby Reid for help with the dyeing of all those gorgeous snow colors. Thanks to my hooking friends for all of their encouragement and suggestions. And, most of all, thanks to my husband, Keith, for the countless hours of joining me on the mountain. His greatest contribution, however, is answering with tact: "How is it looking *now*?"

Downhill, 23" x 22", #3-cut hand-dyed wool with some wool roving and glitter ribbon on monk's cloth. Designed and hooked by Barb Powell, Redmond, Oregon, 2017.

Barb Powell
Redmond, Oregon

Barb previously ran a small wholesale/retail coffee roasting business in Tillamook for sixteen years before retiring with her husband, Keith. She belongs to the Tillamook Rug Crafters, is the past president of ATHA Region 11, and became a McGown Certified Instructor in 2016. This is her first appearance in Celebration.

Fiddler on the Roof

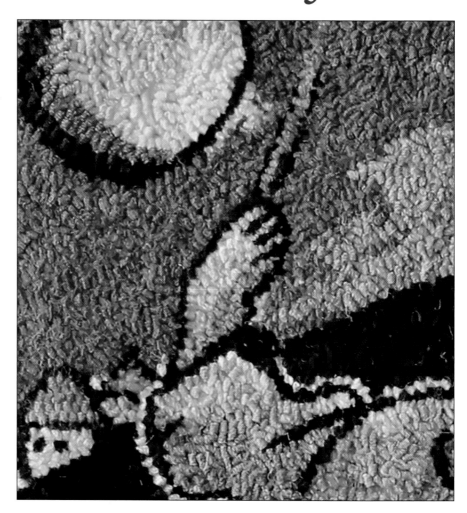

The inspiration for designing this rug came from signing up for a rug hooking class on art "isms," such as modernism, impressionism, cubism, etc. *Fiddler on the Roof* has been an all-time favorite musical for both myself and my husband. He was going to be celebrating his sixty-fifth birthday, and I wanted to make something special for him.

This was the first time I used black as a main color—it did give the piece some drama. The use of bright colors for the fiddler really made him, as well as some of the minor motifs, stand out. I used the "wandering" dye technique for dyeing the rooftops; this gave them a softer blending edge.

I used both new and reclaimed wool. Using new wool, I could dye the bright colors I needed. I had some black wool from a jacket that I used as is. I bled out some of the color in some of the black, and to my happy surprise, it had a blue-gray base and was perfect for the transition from the subtle outline of rooftops to the blackish hills. I also used strands of yellow and green embroidery floss to hook around the menorah tree. This helped to outline and bring it forward.

My favorite part of the piece is the fiddler's face. I love the way his expression evolved and the colors I used to create him. I found his violin to be a bit of a challenge. Tanya Graham, my teacher with this piece, said that the violin looked a bit like a box and that beautiful music was not able to come from it. She suggested that I really accentuate the curvature of the violin. I did, and it looks so much better! The most important thing I learned from this rug was the use of contrast. I used both high and low contrast, which I think contribute to the drama in this piece.

A friend showed me how to pull up my first loop, and since then, I have tried to take a variety of classes to further my knowledge. I enjoy both the solitude and comradeship in rug hooking. I find the act of pulling up loops very meditative. I enjoy the creative aspect as well as being able to personally express myself.

Val Flannigan
Kelowna, British Columbia, Canada

Val is currently retired. She's a member of TIGHR, ATHA, PHRHS, Green Mountain, and Kelowna Traditional Rug Hookers. She has also dabbled in quilting, stitching, beading, knitting, and felting. This is her fifth appearance in Celebration.

Fiddler on the Roof, 16½" x 21½", #4-cut hand-dyed wool on linen. Designed and hooked by Val Flannigan, Kelowna, British Columbia, Canada, 2017. GRAEME FLANNIGAN

Four Seasons

My friend showed me paintings by J.F. Lansdowne, and this inspired me to make a rug with birds. The first rug I made was a wreath for summer with images of birds. I wasn't satisfied because the images were small, and I couldn't put some features on it that I had wanted. The next rug I made was bullfinches in the winter, which gave me the idea to make a bigger rug with scenes of the seasons.

This rug depicts four seasons: Baltimore orioles in summer, woodpeckers on birches in fall under the rain, chickadees in winter, and yellow finches in spring. The motifs on the rug are hooked higher than the background, then each top is clipped to create a relief effect.

I color planned the rug myself. I just pulled pieces from my considerable stash of wool until I was happy with the combination. I hooked the woodpeckers on the birches first.

Once, on a walk in the woods, I saw a woodpecker on a birch branch between yellow leaves. It inspired me, and I was ready to begin the rug. For the winter square, I chose chickadees because they are the most common bird you see in the winter. The spring square needed yellow birds to complement the yellow leaves from the fall square. I chose Baltimore orioles for summer because they have yellow and red colors. To finish the rug, I whipped the edges with wool yarn in such a way that the yarn almost cannot be seen, and finished it with rug tape.

I got started in rug hooking after a friend invited me to the rug-hooking group in Sudbury, Ontario, Canada. Making rugs is more than a hobby for me. I find it's a means of self-expression. Every new rug invites the use of different artistic elements, and I am happy to share my experience with others.

Four Seasons, 32" x 32", #3-cut hand-dyed wool on linen. Designed and hooked by Tatiana Knodel, Sudbury, Ontario, Canada, 2017.

Tatiana Knodel
Sudbury, Ontario, Canada

Tatiana is a scientist with a PhD in chemistry. She is a certified teacher of the Ontario Hooking Craft Guild and belongs to the rug hooking group Rug on the Rocks that meets in Sudbury, Ontario, Canada. This is her fourth appearance in Celebration.

Giverny, France

In 2012, my husband and I took a wonderful trip to Paris, France. We toured the lovely city and countryside with all its splendor. One of the excursions was a tour of Claude Monet's home. I fell in love with the land, pond, and famous green bridge. I knew then that I wanted to capture the essence of the Impressionist art form in a rug. Upon our return, as we were reviewing my husband's photos of the trip, we both fell for this street scene. We adapted the photo with an Impressionist styling, and it was then that I was on a mission to complete my floor-size rug.

After taking a class from Capri Boyle Jones, my palette of wool was reviewed and broadened to accommodate the elements and light sources in the design. I bundled wool into packages of color for the specific areas and to manage hooking time efficiently.

I choose to work with light, medium, and dark values more than any one color. The reasoning behind that is to play with the way light affects objects; light has a way of changing colors we see with the naked eye. I wanted to keep the light source and textures in mind when working with this design.

It's hard to say what part of the piece I love the most, but I would go with the buildings. I worked a lot on the shading, textures, and directional hooking to keep movement and interest while sticking to the Impressionist style.

The road was, no doubt, a challenge. Since the road has a prominent placement in the design, I knew the color needed to be subtle but strong enough to hold weight and keep the eye moving about in the design. The color had to be different than the buildings, too, so as not to compete or take attention away. Directional hooking played a key role to maintain the curve and lead you into the background.

With this rug, I learned that scale and proportion in a large rug is a huge deal. I also need to keep in mind what steps I needed to take to keep the design perspective, how important it was to keep the rug out all the time, and what roles sunlight, or lack thereof, played on the colors.

In The Judges' Eyes: *Painterly approach to shading and lighting; Impressionism in wool, quite the challenge; Very good impressionist hooking.*

Giverny, France, 57¼" x 45¼", #7- to 8.5-cut wool on linen. Designed and hooked by Sheri Ahner, Kirkwood, Missouri, 2017. GARRY MCMICHAEL

Sheri Ahner
Kirkwood, Missouri

Sheri is an account manager for a large exhibit company. She also processes and dyes sheep fiber for hand-spinning art yarns, either to knit with or to add as other wool elements in newly designed rugs. This is her first entry into any competition and her first appearance in Celebration.

Halloween Mischief

My husband and I have always liked vintage Halloween motifs, and I began to imagine a cemetery setting with witches and a cauldron. The initials in four of the tombstones represent deceased persons special to me: my father, a rug-hooking friend from Montana, a software mentor, and a fellow antiques dealer.

I used some dip-dyed materials for the witches' clothing and to create a more realistic fire. Teacher Ingrid Hieronimus offered a wonderful dip-dyed piece ranging from yellow to purple to create a very effective glowing night sky, which really shows off the many images against it. An all–dark blue or purple sky wouldn't have let the images stand out as they do now against the yellow-to-purple part of the sky. Some interesting purple wools and some spot-dyed purple wools gave the darker part of the sky more movement and eye appeal.

The color for the large area of grass was a soft and paler yellow-green plaid with some light brown areas. That wool better reflected the fall time period for the piece than using brighter or darker greens. Choosing a color for the horse was interesting. I ruled out black and brown because of so much other use of those colors in the witch hats, cauldron, cat, tombstones, stone wall, and dirt path. A white horse seemed too bright for the piece. So I thought of roan horses and dapple gray horses. I had fun creating the wool for a dapple gray horse by creating wool with salt-shaker dyeing and then spotting some of it with very weak black dye.

I had bought and sold hooked rugs in my thirty-year career, along with quilts, coverlets, samples, and more in the German area of Pennsylvania where I lived. I'd never even considered rug hooking and knew nothing about it.

Then in 2003 or 2004, a copy of *Rug Hooking* magazine was displayed in a holder on the wall of a store at eye level. I bought that copy and read through it and was intrigued enough to subscribe. I've now hooked well over fifty rugs, several of them quite large. I like the creativeness in making designs I like—usually inspired by antique items or by cartoons. I also enjoy "being in control" of my materials and colors by learning many different dyeing techniques, using dyes from several different companies, and using many different books for dye formulas.

Halloween Mischief, 51½" x 52", #3- to 5-cut hand-dyed and as-is wool on monk's cloth. Designed and hooked by Susan Cunningham, Laramie, Wyoming, 2017. DAVID CUNNINGHAM

Susan Cunningham
Laramie, Wyoming

Susan is retired from being a software developer and owner of a business that sold a commercial software product used in over one thousand stores nationwide. This is her fifth appearance in Celebration.

He Holds All Creation Together

This rug was inspired by the beautiful words of the poem found in the first chapter of Colossians in the New Living Translation (1:15–20). While sitting in church one day, I sketched the idea for this rug, with the cross representing Jesus Christ in the background like a watermark. It was a very rudimentary sketch. Planning to go to Gene Shepherd's California getaway, I consulted with Gene, who gave me the idea of starting with "chaos." And when I got to Anaheim, Gene took me to Kinko's, where they were able to blow up my little 2" x 3" sketch into the full-size pattern that I envisioned for my rug. When I thought of an animal that I wanted to include, I would search for images of that animal and then practice drawing the animal on paper before adding it to the rug. It was challenging but also a lot of fun.

I wanted to include some animals that I just liked, as well as some animals that I had seen when I went to Africa, like the elephants and lion. The elephants were very challenging because they were, of necessity, smaller. They did not show up well against the sky color I was using, so I decided to place them against a deep "sunset" color. And I chose to include a macaw because long ago, my brother and I had a pet shop, and we had a macaw as the shop mascot.

Originally I had my mind set on using a bright yellow for the cross. But in spite of repeated dye efforts, nothing seemed to work. Finally I found a lovely soft golden color (dyed by Gene) that was perfect. Keeping the cross in the background and yet clearly visible was a challenge, but I'm pleased with how that turned out.

I had admired rug hooking for a long time, and one day, I decided I wanted to try it. I contacted Gene Shepherd about going to Cambria Pines Rug Camp, and he steered me to my first rug-hooking teacher, Carol Pinkins, so I would have a basic knowledge of rug hooking before I came to camp. Carol was a great teacher. If not for her determination, I might not have continued rug hooking!

Debby Schnabel
Pine Grove, California

Debby is a retired neonatal intensive care nurse who now works full-time on her art quilts and part-time on her rug hooking. He Holds All Creation Together *was displayed at the Cambria Pines Rug Show. This is her first appearance in* Celebration.

He Holds All Creation Together, 28" x 47", #6-cut hand-dyed wool on linen. Designed and hooked by Debby Schnabel, Pine Grove, California, 2016.

Honest Eds

Honest Eds was one of my favorite places in the city of Toronto. You could count on always getting a bargain. It was retail therapy before the term was coined. As a student, most of my wardrobe was from Honest Eds. My first set of dishes came from Honest Eds. While I was in art college, I bought SX-70 film and Kodachrome there. In line at the cash register, you could peruse the goods of other shoppers. Many were immigrants outfitting their first homes in Canada with sheets, towels, brightly colored enamel pots and pans, and plastic doilies. It was always interesting and a different slice of life from my own. My rug also has a Hero hamburger sign, which reminds me of what a true hero of Toronto Ed Mirvish (a.k.a. Honest Ed) was. He bought and restored the Royal Alexandra Theater and built the Princess of Wales Theatre. He rescued Markham Street and turned it into Mirvish Village. It became a street of chic boutiques, quaint restaurants, art galleries, bookstores, and clubs with live music. Alas, Honest Eds is no more. Flatbed trucks came and carted away the circus-like sign. Scaffolding has been put up, and the store is ready for demolition. New condos will replace Honest Eds, but they won't replace the memories in the hearts of Torontonians.

I chose the colors to match a photograph that I had taken of the store. I did quite a bit of dyeing for this piece. I painted the dye onto the wool for the

background of the sign. I used three Maryanne Lincoln formulas—Rusty Tulip, Butterscotch, and Rich Red—for the faded sign. I pleated and dyed the wool for the corrugated metal (blue and gray striped bits). This is known as shibori technique. I sprinkled a mixture of salt and black dye for the dark parts of the streetcar. I used old plaid cashmere scarves for most of the reflections in the store window and a blue tweed cashmere scarf for the front window of the streetcar.

I was hoping to have this rug ready to go to the Ontario Hooking Craft Guild's Annual last year in Cobourg, but I would have had to rush. I asked myself, "What is the priority here—that my rug goes to the annual or that I feel that I've done the best that I could?" I spent about a month tweaking it after I had finished hooking it, and I think that was a good idea.

In The Judges' Eyes: *A complicated design executed masterfully. Reflection in every section adds to the story; Images distorted by glass and glare add to the busy scene, yet most signs are easily readable. The sign saying ANYPLACE! is especially telling. This is a common sort of urban scene that could indeed be any place.*

Trish Johnson
Toronto, Ontario, Canada

Aside from being a rug hooker, Trish is a quilter, photographer, wife, mother, and grandmother. She's won Rug Hooking Artist of the Year (Canadian) at the Rug Hooking Museum of North America and the Rowan Award (Best of Show), Original Award, and Pictorial Award at the Ontario Hooking Craft Guild's Annual. This is her twelfth appearance in Celebration.

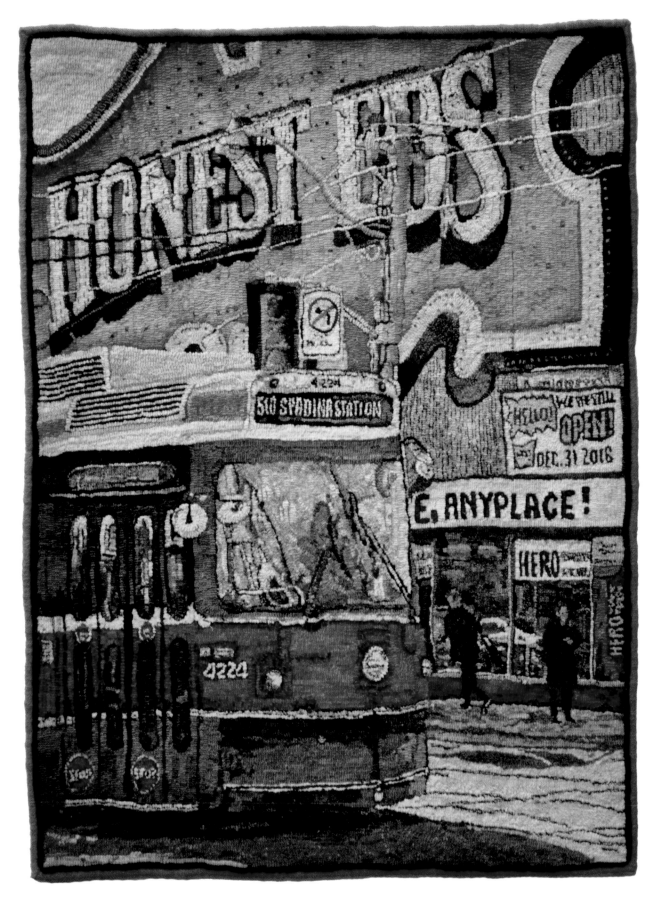

Honest Eds, 25¼" x 34", #3- to 5-cut wool with some strands of woolen yarn on linen. Designed and hooked by Trish Johnson, Toronto, Ontario, Canada, 2017.

Liberty

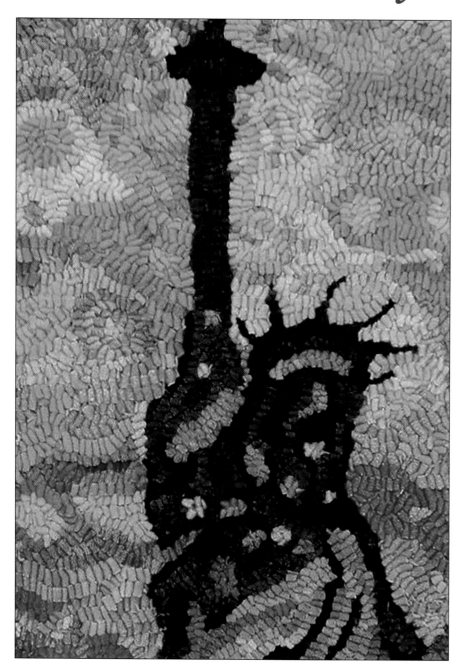

I designed a series of famous and cherished country symbols in a highly stylized format, including *Liberty*, *Eiffel Tower*, and *Leaning Tower of Pisa*. This began as a black-and-white photograph that I colored. The intention was to do something very different with the statue [who is she?] using deep jewel tones and pastel colors in a contemporary design.

I primarily used wool for this rug, with some yarn and ribbons for highlights and fiber variety. I didn't want to do a typical blue sky, and I wanted high contrast with the sky and statue, so I created highly spot-dyed wool fabric. I dye almost all of my wool myself, but I also purchase wool from very good dyers.

My favorite part of this rug is the face. Even though it's stylized, it's truly welcoming. The left arm and hand were the most difficult because the scroll wasn't very clear. It required smaller cuts to get the look right. To finish the rug, I whipped rug yarn around the edges.

A friend took me to a hook-in seven years ago, and I've been rug hooking ever since. I love that it allows me creative freedom and style, and I really like experimentation. This rug taught me how emotional rugs can be while working on them.

> **In The Judges' Eyes:** *Not what we would expect in coloring, which makes it even more powerful; Colorful and creative. A black silhouette would be ho-hum. The colors within the statue rock this piece.*

Sharon A. Smith
Walnut Creek, California

Sharon is a psychologist. She's also involved in knitting, quilting, punch needle, and wool appliqué. She's a member of ATHA. This is her second appearance in Celebration.

Liberty, 18" x 28", wool on linen. Designed and hooked by Sharon A. Smith, Walnut Creek, California, 2017.

Morning Haze

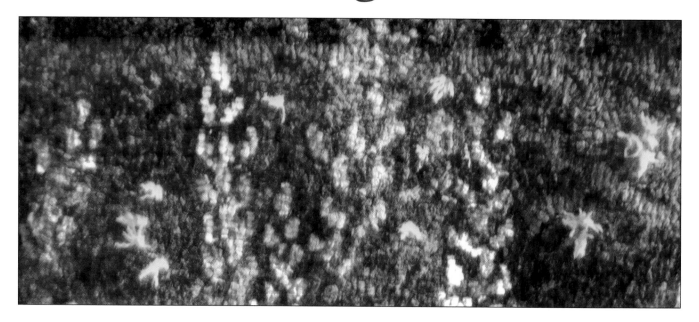

The origin of this rug came from when I drew a simple pattern of a lighthouse and water on burlap for a friend. Due to problems with her wrist, she was unable to hook it, so I bought it back, left it for a few years, and then decided to hook it. I redrew the whole thing to suit me, and as I hooked, I kept adding things—my nephew's lobster boat, lupins, seagulls, rocks—until it was pleasing to my eye.

I dyed most of the wool myself and tried a few different colors for the water and sky. They were the hardest colors to choose. I wanted both the water and sky to be darker than on a sunny day. The sky is partly dip-dyed for the horizon. I think it makes it look like there is an impending storm coming. The clouds are spot dyes I did, with other grays mixed in.

I'm biased because I like the whole rug together, but I do have a couple of favorite spots. I was hooking the front grass and cliff, and when I stepped back to look at it, it seemed to have a 3-D effect, as though it was popping out from the lighthouse. I wondered how I did that, but I liked the effect. Adding my nephew's lobster boat seemed to finish it off. The surf around the rocks, trying to make it look like water, was challenging to do, as was hooking the rocks. I just worked through it until it felt right.

Both my aunt and mother designed and hooked their own rugs. I always thought when I retired, I would get them to teach me, but alas, my aunt died in 1990 and my mother in 1994, both from cancer. In 1994, our doctor's wife offered to teach me, so I took her up on it, and the rest is history. I've taken a few classes at the rug hooking school offered by the Rug Hooking Guild of Nova Scotia, as well as a few workshops. I think rug hooking is the most relaxing and forgiving hobby that I have done. I get to design my own rugs and paint with wool at the same time. I dabble as a watercolorist also and am amazed at some of the effects I can get with fiber.

> **In The Judges' Eyes:** *Consistent attention to light source with the white waves adding interest, connecting the bird to lighthouse; The sky is wonderful and the lupins in the foreground are the exclamation point. All-around nice rug. Great sky, creates a feeling of the shoreline after a rainstorm.*

Toni Gallagher
Annapolis Royal, Nova Scotia, Canada

Toni is retired. She belongs to the Rug Hooking Guild of Nova Scotia Fundy Group, which meets once a month, and to three other smaller groups that hook one day every week. This is her third appearance in Celebration.

Morning Haze, 31" x 27", #3-cut hand-dyed wool on burlap. Designed and hooked by Toni Gallagher, Annapolis Royal, Nova Scotia, Canada, 2016.

Mosaic Muse

I have mentioned to a few people that color planning is not a comfortable process for me. To be very honest, it's downright painful. I ultimately end up with a rug design that I'm fairly satisfied with, but there is a lot of sweat and tears (and reverse hooking!) before I get there. I thought it would be fun and relaxing to work on something with a repetitive pattern and constant color plan for a change. I was ready to design a geometric rug! My search for inspiration led me to a wonderful world of mosaic art. It was there that I found a simple mosaic leaf that inspired the rest of this rug.

Most of my rug hooking has been on monk's cloth. I wanted this rug to be symmetrical, so I was counting threads to make sure certain areas were equal. However, because of the weave of my monk's cloth, this was distorting the design. The problem was easily solved by moving the design to linen. This was the first rug that I was able to complete using wool that I had on hand. I chose the wools based on color and texture and used mostly as-is wool.

I envisioned most of the colors as I was drawing up the design. One of my favorite choices was using two different browns in the background, which created the subtle square within the squares. I'm not sure that I have a favorite section of this rug, but I love beading and the whimsy it adds to a design. I also had fun letting the design dictate the corners of this rug.

I love creating and have been drawn to many different media over my lifetime. The look and feel of hooked rugs appealed to me long before I picked up a hook. By the time I found the perfect teacher, my heart was already all in. I enjoy many aspects of rug hooking, but I especially enjoy the tactile feel of the wool and the rhythm of the hooking. I have a hard time sitting still unless I'm reading or working on a craft. Rug hooking can be very calming. I also love the variety of styles and personalities that can be found in any group of hookers and their rugs.

In The Judges' Eyes: *Well balanced, and the beading adds interest and a lighter effect than a solid border would. The finish adds a crisp edge to a well-crafted piece; Well thought out. Good use of a variety of textures. Beading is used well, and it is a comfortable piece to view; Pleasant rug with terrific corners.*

Shawn Bybee Niemeyer
Centennial, Colorado

Shawn hooks with a couple of small groups and belongs to the Colorado Rug and Fiber Guild, her local ATHA chapter. She is also learning wool appliqué. This is her third appearance in Celebration.

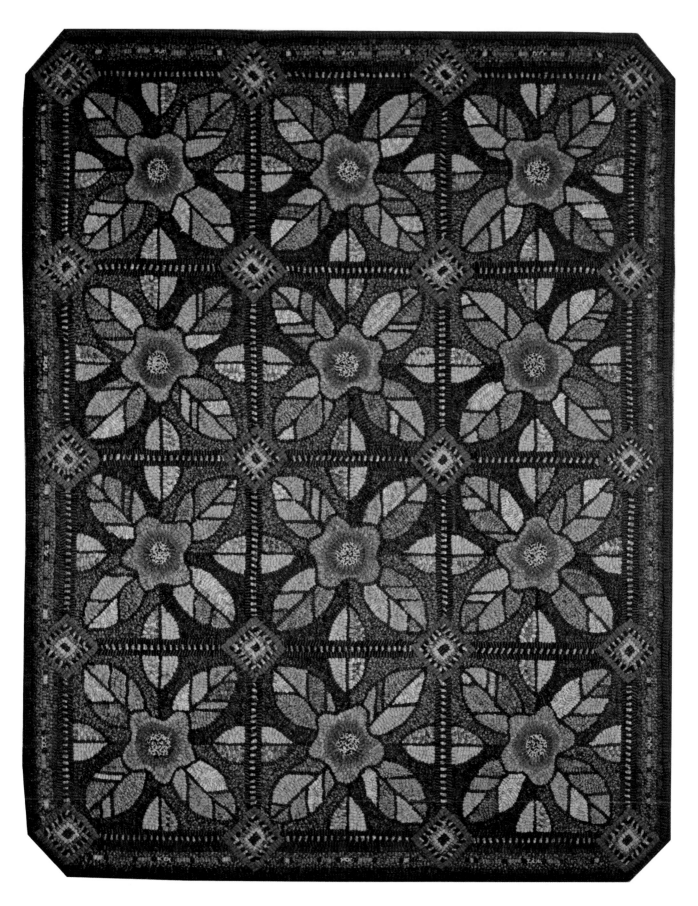

Mosaic Muse, 40" x 32", #4-, 6- and 8-cut as-is wool on linen. Designed and hooked by Shawn Bybee Niemeyer, Centennial, Colorado, 2017. SHAWN BYBEE NIEMEYER AND M.W. BLANTON

No Greater Love

achieve the range of values, I dyed eight half-yard pieces of white wool from the lightest to the darkest values, using a single dye color.

My mother was wearing a plaid blouse, and it was a complicated design to hook. I just worked from my original line drawing and hooked a section at a time, so it would be cohesive and consistent. I learned that hooking plaid is harder than it looks. My favorite part is our two faces, with my mom gazing down at me. I really wanted to capture the expressions on our faces, and that's something that defines the whole purpose of the rug. I was glad it worked.

I have been an artist all my life and explored many different art media. I was introduced to rug hooking by my friends and resisted for a while, but I eventually gave in and, of course, fell in love with it. I love rug hooking because it allows me to express my artistic style in a unique way. I love the texture, the design process, and the ways to explore color and value. There seems to be limitless possibilities, and I have rugs waiting in my mind that are yet to be realized. I need more time!

This rug is based on a photograph my father took of my mother and me when I was six months old, back in August 1958. I wanted to capture the feeling of that moment. I like to think of it as a piece that connects my mother and me, and my father, too, because he captured on film a very special love between us in that moment. By doing so, he expressed his love for us as well.

I hooked the rug with hand-dyed wool in a #3 cut, using a monochromatic color scheme on bleached linen. I love a fine cut because it lets me hook very detailed elements and gives me a greater control of my line. I chose to do a monochromatic purple scheme. The rug features lilacs, my mom's favorite flowers, so the color contributed to the design. I've hooked monochromatic rugs before, but never in purple, so it was fun to play with. To

> **In The Judges' Eyes:** *The dye pot provided the materials, the subject is evoked by the composition, and the master worked the loops; Superb detail in a monochromatic piece. Effective checked background; Lovely expressive rug. Nice monochromatic shading and interesting background.*

Donna Hrkman
Dayton, Ohio

Donna is a fine artist, rug hooker, and rug-hooking teacher. She is the author of Creative Techniques for Rug Hookers *and* Rug Hooker's Companion. *She's also won awards at Sauder Village and Green Mountain at Shelburne. This is her eleventh appearance in* Celebration.

No Greater Love, 22½" x 30", #3-cut hand-dyed wool on bleached linen. Designed and hooked by Donna Hrkman, Dayton, Ohio, 2017. DAN HRKMAN

Oh Starry Night

For this rug camp project, I knew that I wanted to hook a footstool. I scouted out all the antique malls and shops in my area, but I didn't find quite what I was looking for. I did, however, find a nice storage ottoman at a chain store, which had a wool-blend cover. I thought this would be perfect to slip a rug hooking project over, with the wools "holding hands" so to speak. The pieces fit snugly enough that I did not need to tack the hooked pieces to the ottoman fabric itself.

The thrifty and eco-conscious aspects of using recycled wool are appealing to me. They also help me to feel a link to someone in the past who wore or used the wool with which I am hooking, even if I never knew the person. Thus the navy plaid recycled wool fabrics used in my night sky were my actual starting point. I appreciated the thin rows of yellow, green, and red, which were present in the navy plaids and helped all the parts of the project to blend well together. While I love wider-cut rug hooking, I believe my design and color choices are more along the folk-art style than the primitive style. I admire the fine-cut rug hooking of others, but I like to see the actual loops in my personal projects.

I am pleased with how "fussy cutting" the recycled texture for the owl helped to create his wing feathers and body, the bolder plaid used in the roof formed a slate-like effect, and the tiny specks of fireflies near the house evoke many warm, outdoor family memories. I had to hook the path to the house several times before finding a method and texture that worked. I struggled with it just looking like a concrete slab. The foreshortened rock path now appears more natural and in keeping with the cottage.

My mother, Arline Johnstone, is a McGown Certified Instructor. My daughter, Nicole Cunningham, had been hooking with Grandma for quite a number of years. They finally convinced me to get a project started with the idea that, if I enjoyed it, we would all go to rug camp together. My mom and daughter were both available to answer my questions, so I got off to a great start! I love the textile arts, such as weaving, knitting, spinning, and rug hooking. I also love the "stitch" definition you see when hooking wider-cut strips, which can be almost impressionistic in style. There really is something special about working with wool!

Donna Cunningham
Muncie, Indiana

Donna currently works in the Center for Autism at Ball State University and has been a special education teacher in the past. This project has been shown as a returning completed project at the Tomorrow's Heirlooms rug camp show in Holland, Michigan. This is her first appearance in Celebration.

Oh Starry Night, 17" x 17", #6- to 8-cut hand-dyed, recycled, and as-is wool on linen. Designed and hooked by Donna Cunningham, Muncie, Indiana, 2016.

Ricker Lobster Company

Before this rug, I had only hooked floral patterns. I wanted a change and felt the photos of our commercial lobster business would offer the opportunity for an interesting and meaningful pictorial. Once all the scenes were chosen, the final layout began. Balance of shape and color finally came together with the guidance of Lois Dugal, my instructor. This was an enormous learning experience that I would not have attempted without her advisement.

The pattern for each scene came from paintings, photos, and old postcards. My friend and professional artist, Wendy Hazen, had done a painting of our lobster boat, Early Dawn. She was very excited to have her rendition be one of the center scenes. Our business, Ricker Lobster Company, located right on the dock, became the other focal point. The Fort Point Lighthouse was my most difficult section because of the perspective. I wanted to illustrate the curvature of the building but maintain the proper values. The rocks were rehooked several times to achieve the illusion of individual rocks. The lobster buoys in the upper left-hand corner

presented the same challenge regarding perspective. My "signature" is always a hummingbird, so the beach rose was a must.

I wanted the sky and water of each section to be quite different. The spot-dyed swatches made that much easier. It also became the answer for achieving weathered wood. My favorite section is the lobster pound. The building and road offered an opportunity to use shading techniques I had learned for florals but now worked to show depth down the road and emphasize the shapes and shadows of the buildings. I finished the rug by turning the burlap to the back, whipstitching a very narrow edge, and adding tape.

As a young girl, I watched my grandmother and her friends working on their rugs in her living room. Who would have guessed that fifty years later I would be doing the same, using her Puritan frame, Fraser cutter, and hooks. With this rug, I learned that I really enjoy designing my own pattern. I loved hooking the landscape and structures, and I am looking forward to another project that will show our life and memories.

In The Judges' Eyes: *I want to visit. An artist was in the dye pot. The backgrounds are complicated, setting the mood of each motif. Good balance in composition; A lot of story in a small piece; Beautiful story rug. Excellent shading. Very soft and painterly.*

Janis Ricker
Portsmouth, New Hampshire

Janis is a retired lobster dealer and part-time lobster fisher. She is a member of the Mayflower ATHA group in Massachusetts and Seacoast Hookers in Kittery, Maine. This is her first appearance in Celebration.

Ricker Lobster Company, 42½" x 26", #3- and 4-cut hand-dyed wool on burlap. Designed and hooked by Janis Ricker, Portsmouth, New Hampshire, 2016. LISANNE MILLER

Speaking Shakespeare

I was inspired to create this rug after I saw some posts on Pinterest with common phrases used by Shakespeare in his plays that are still in use today. I had an idea to do a rug with a few of the phrases and asked Ellen Banker, a graphic designer, to lay out the phrases in a design for a rug. Before I knew it, the project had expanded to include an image of Shakespeare, then grew substantially in size to increase the font to something I could hook.

I used nine values of a sepia-colored wool, plus the same color dyed over a texture for the doublet. I wanted the background to have a parchment look to it and used the lightest value there. I also used monk's cloth as the backing, so I could split threads and put the hook exactly where I needed it for the detailed script. To finish the rug, I whipped the edge with matching wool cut in #8 strips, so it would blend in with the border.

The whole image of the head was a challenge because of the larger-than-life size. When I was ready to start, I was taking a class with Donna Hrkman, and she was very helpful with suggestions. My favorite part of the rug is the eyes; I feel I was successful in portraying them.

The biggest thing I learned from this rug is not to be afraid of lettering! It was daunting to start, but once I figured it out, it really wasn't that difficult.

I first got started in rug hooking when I was on a house tour in Portsmouth, New Hampshire, in the early 1990s. I saw a house full of hooked rugs and decided I had to learn how to make them. I enjoy rug hooking because it's relaxing, it's portable, and it allows for a lot of travel to meet up with other rug hookers.

In The Judges' Eyes: *The palette, the composition, the choice of font, and the values from dye pot all come together; Fabulous hooked, script lettering. Good job on the face and beard.*

Marian Hall
West Chester, Pennsylvania

Marian is a retired occupational therapist who now has a small business dyeing wool, Wooly Dye Works. She belongs to ATHA, the Brandywine Rug Hooking Guild, the Hunterdon County Rug Artisans Guild, the Mason Dixon Guild, and TIGHR. This is her fourth appearance in Celebration.

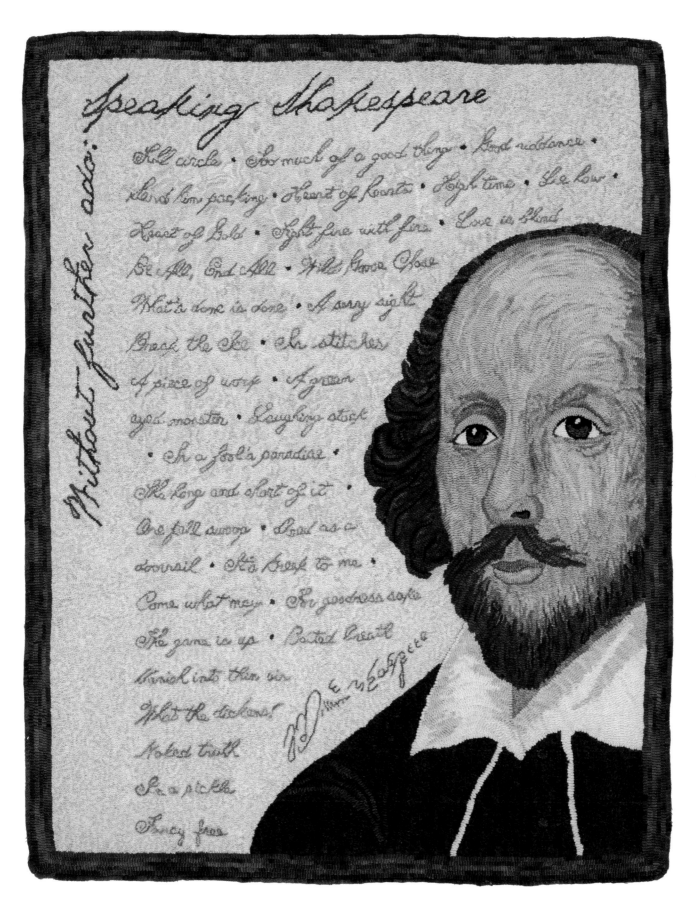

Speaking Shakespeare, 36½" x 47", #2- to 6-cut hand-dyed wool on monk's cloth. Designed by Marian Hall and Ellen Banker and hooked by Marian Hall, West Chester, Pennsylvania, 2017. LYNN BOHANNON AND MARIAN HALL

Temple Fish

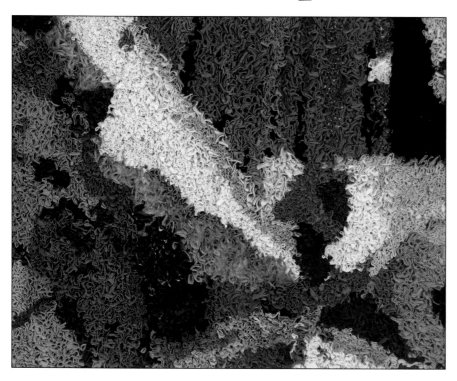

In mid-2016, I was in Bali teaching a two-week workshop at the Gaya Ceramic Arts Centre. It was an intensive workshop involving international participants working on multiple firings. After we'd completed the final firing, the Gaya staff took us to a local water temple for a day of cooling, contemplation, and cultural experience. Visually, there was a feast of color and movement, including a pool of brightly-colored koi carp. I knew immediately there would be rugs to follow from the photos I took.

I enjoy the challenge of working with reclaimed fabric. Sourcing material, creating a palette, and adapting to the needs of the design require a degree of inventiveness and contribute to the variety of color and texture. I made this rug entirely with fabric strips, using "shorn proggy" technique. The trimmed open pile creates a shimmering effect similar to the water's surface.

I enjoy the large solid areas of red, blue, and black in the right-hand half of the rug. The shading there gives an eye-catching sense of three dimensions and provides balance to the more complex, detailed areas of the design. The rippled rings in the upper left-hand corner were challenging because they involved such a high degree of detail. I paid careful attention to the photo I was working from and sketched in the detail as I worked, changing colors frequently as required. Patience and persistence paid off as, bit by bit, the image came together.

In 2014, my friend and neighbor Maggie Hickey ran a small rug-making workshop in her studio, and I attended—primarily to be sociable. But I became hooked! Maggie and I later attended some gatherings of the Narrawilly Proggy Ruggers at Miriam Miller's studio in Milton, New South Wales. I bought my first rugging frame from Miriam. She and her group were very supportive of my efforts. Shortly after I started rug hooking, I visited an Arthur Boyd exhibition at the National Gallery of Australia. In the final room of that show, I encountered a series of tapestries Boyd had commissioned to be made in Portugal from his pastel drawings. Those tapestries were so vibrant and powerful, I was inspired to explore the artistic potential of the rug-making techniques I was learning.

From the beginning of my rug hooking, I was intrigued by the freedom of design and the suitability of this medium for abstract work. Although I loved my previous ceramic work, I am amazed at how naturally the transition between media occurred. It was as if thirty years working professionally in ceramics had prepared me for this new artistic challenge, and it was time to move on. I feel blessed to have discovered this new direction in my work, and the support amongst the rug hooking community.

Gail Nichols
Braidwood, New South Wales, Australia

Gail was a professional ceramic artist for thirty years who now primarily focuses on textile art. This rug was exhibited at her solo exhibition of textiles and ceramics, "In Transit," at the Drill Hall Gallery of the Australian National University in Canberra in June and July 2018. This is her first appearance in Celebration.

Temple Fish, 62" x 45", new and recycled fabrics on hessian burlap. Designed and hooked by Gail Nichols. Braidwood, New South Wales, Australia, 2017.

In The Judges' Eyes: *The texture of clipped ends (prodded) add softness to the angular design. Clean transition from one shape/space to the next. The reds draw me around the design; Exquisitely done proddy and use of various fabrics. Nice movement and texture throughout.*

The Fish Carpet

I was inspired to create this rug from memories of my dad. He was the consummate fisherman, from lake trout in the Eastern Townships to beautiful speckled trout caught both in the provincial parks of northern Quebec and at his fishing camp that he shared with his brothers and other friends. Fishing represented times that mattered in life. Fishing set the course. The fish in the carpet is the fish of my father's dreams.

I started with the fish and was influenced by photos of real trout. I think the black and white– and sepia-toned photos caused me to continue with a rather subdued palette. I needed to separate the fish from the rest of the story, hence the blues, greens, and purples. I dyed most of the wool for the fish but also worked with many casserole-dyed pieces and swatches made by some very talented dyers in our community.

I love the face of the fish and the surrounding water. For one, fish bite when it's cloudy. But I think, more importantly, his angry face is defying anyone to catch him. As with most rugs, the further you go with the rug, the harder it gets. Each section interacts with the next. The water was the greatest challenge, and it was the last thing I worked on.

Working in a #3 cut allowed me to become more articulate and detailed. I've always loved rug hooking. We had a piece in our house hooked by my grandmother's nanny from Cape Breton

Island, made from a Garrett Bluenose pattern. It used flat, colored yarn. When I saw that you could shade colors with various dyeing techniques, I was thrilled at the possibilities.

I worked on cotton warp, which withstood the test of time. The rug took me twenty-four years to complete. I'm pretty sure burlap would not have met the challenge. I love rug warp. It's soft and yet tight enough to hold the stitches.

I've always loved fiber. I've been knitting and crocheting since I was a child. I tried my hand at spinning and weaving but failed miserably. I think weaving is too structured, too much advanced thinking for me. Rug hooking offered me the flexibility and a different

kind of control than all the others. When making this rug, I learned that I am stubborn and have willpower. I learned that all those years of studying art and film were worth it. I learned that I have great friends who supported me every step along the way.

In The Judges' Eyes: *Color where needed, neutrals emphasize the nostalgia. The outer border does just what a frame should—enhance the subject. Painterly use of values develops the vignettes; A rug hooking story par excellence, visually moving from story to story, wonderful workmanship, creative and a masterpiece.*

Peggy Peacock
Toronto, Ontario, Canada

Peggy is an events producer, working on corporate sales meetings, product launches, trade shows, and street festivals. The Fish Carpet *won the Best Original Category and the People's Choice Award at the Ontario Hooked Craft Guild Annual in 2016 and was featured in the 2017 fall edition of* ATHA *magazine. This is her first appearance in* Celebration.

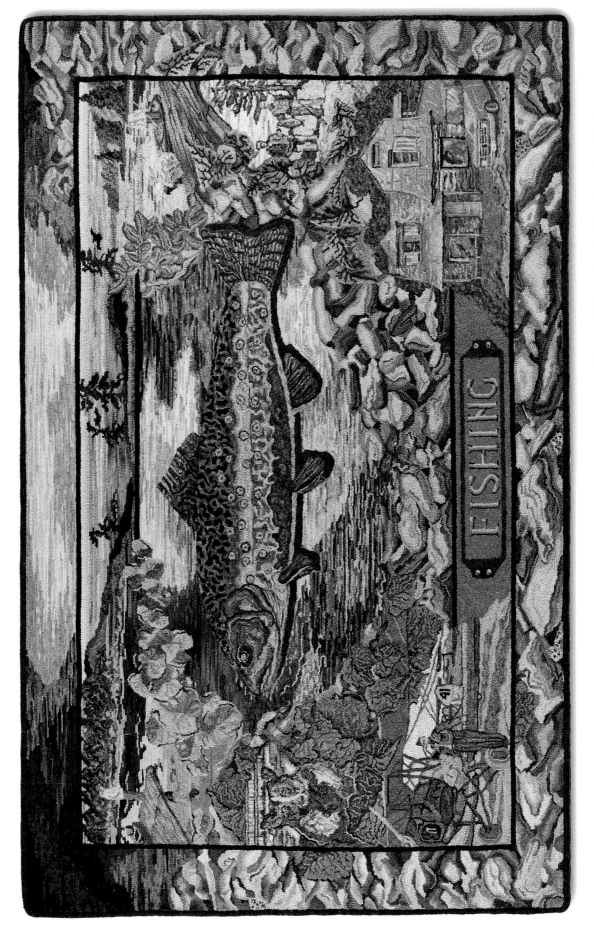

The Fish Carpet, 72" x 48", #3-cut wool on cotton rug warp. Designed and hooked by Peggy Peacock, Toronto, Ontario, Canada. 2016. MATHEW PLEXMAN

Zoo Day

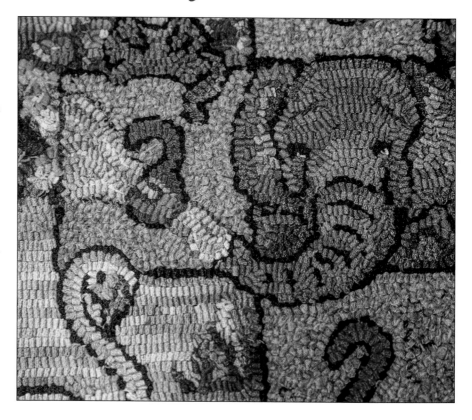

This rug was a gift for my new granddaughter, Arden, born in 2016. My son and family live near Audubon Zoo in New Orleans, and they will pack their little red wagon with Arden and big sister, Tallie, and spend the day with friends, exploring the zoo. When Tallie was born, I had adapted a commercial pattern and used the alphabet for a border, but for Arden's rug, I wanted to use numbers. My daughter came up with the idea of using the hopscotch layout as a way of moving through the zoo and ending at a wonderful play area called Monkey Hill.

I wanted the colors to reflect a bright, clear day. Most of the wool was from my stash, both off-the-bolt and hand-dyed. I did dip dye the grass so that I could control the light and dark areas around the motifs. I decided to outline the motifs so that I would not have to be too concerned with the placing of similar values together.

I had never hooked animals before, so I was apprehensive. I tend to hook birds and flowers, so when I got to the elephant, I knew that this would be my challenge. The elephant hooked up so easily that I had no qualms about continuing. I decided to give him a friend, the mouse, and then the flowers needed watering, so I added the elephant watering the flowers. It all just came together and was a lot of fun to hook.

In 1967, my husband-to-be took me to meet his mother. Ruth had hooked rugs for a long time and showed me the process. I had done needlework, knitting, crochet, and sewing for a long time, but I had never seen anything like hooking. She took used clothing, cut

it up with scissors, and made beautiful rugs. Whenever I visited, Ruth and I would take turns hooking and cutting fabric. It was a most enjoyable time. Ruth passed in 1972, but I kept her hook with the dog's teeth marks in the handle and use it exclusively to hook. It just feels right.

Rug hooking connects me to the past; it grounds me. I love reading and hearing about other rug hookers, past and present. Also, I love color. Some people seem to have an innate ability to use color, and then there are those of us who

have to study and work to understand it. Hooking is one of the best ways that I have found to study color.

In The Judges' Eyes: *Especially liked the coloring for water spewing from elephant's trunk. Lots to learn in this design; Well done, everything a little one would love and learn about, nice coloration and rug hooking; Very cute rug. Wonderful hooking job, great colors, and lots of pretty detail.*

Janet Hamstead
Mount Vernon, Ohio

Janet is primarily a homemaker and mother but also holds a BS in Biology and an MFA and has taught part-time at West Virginia State and Marshall Universities. She has a varied interest in art and tries everything from colored pencils to mosaics but always comes back to fiber and needle arts. This is her first appearance in Celebration.

Zoo Day, 18" x 42", #3- to 6-cut wool on linen. Designed and hooked by Janet Hamstead, Mount Vernon, Ohio, 2017. CALEB MCCOY

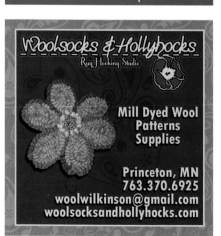

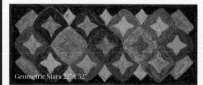

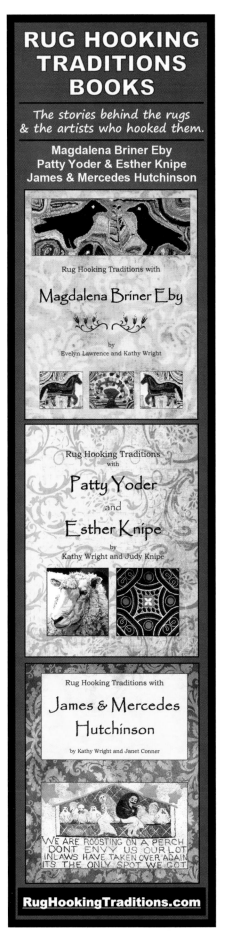

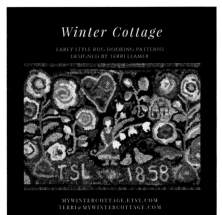

Alphapets

It's all about love, isn't it? Look at God's creation, and you can see how much love went into each and every step of it. The animals each have their own personalities. Some live independently yet depend on each other for food, shelter, and procreation. *Alphapets*, to me, captures the ultimate in a variety of animal characteristics. My goal in creating and imagining each precious creation was to instill in our grandson the beauty of God's creation and His love for us through nature.

This rug is dedicated to my mom, Ruth Dietzel, and her extraordinary gift of art through "painting with wool." Mom's first gift of love to me began as I listened and learned at her feet, learning of the world as the purr of the sewing machine translated miles of fabric and thread into clothes such as gowns, suits, and slacks. Fast-forward to rug hooking: her eye for color piqued my curiosity as I studied the sunlight and how it danced on leaves and tree trunks, animal fur, and wings of birds.

I chose animal colors based on their individual characteristics, and background colors indicative of the animals' habitat. By considering the animal's color, I considered seasonal differences and went with the best match for that particular view. For the swatched colors, I used the jar-dyeing method. Other important considerations involved the "look" of the panels to the naked eye. Where was the interest drawn for each horizontal panel? Where was the balance of color in another area of the rug? How were the backgrounds destined to flow?

Do I color outside the lettering or not?

The elephant is my favorite section of the piece. As the largest land mammals, they are extremely intelligent; the leaders often guide the herd to necessary food during dry seasons. As I hooked the shades of gray, I thought about the awesome responsibility of parenting and grandparenting those we leave behind. The most challenging part of the rug was the antelope. I had no problem with his gorgeous horns, but the body proportions were a struggle for me. My teacher, Karen Maddox, guided me through all of it.

My mom introduced me to rug hooking when I was thirty-five years old (seemingly eons ago). With her gift to me of Pearl McGown's book on color, I was "hooked." Rug hooking provides me with a special respite. Whether I am in a group of fellow artisans or alone, I think about the many facets of this traditional art. I revel in God's beauty from the very fibers of the lamb's wool, the processing from shearing to spinning to the weaving of the fibers, and more than that, to the warmth and loft it provides.

Donna M. Stone
The Hills, Texas

Donna is a mother, grandmother, retired Air Force nurse, pastoral health minister, Bible study teacher, and singer. She's also involved in sewing, quilting, knitting, crocheting, needlepoint, ikebana (Japanese flower arranging), and sumi brush painting. This is her first appearance in Celebration.

Alphapets, 32½" x 56", #3- and 4-cut wool on linen. Designed by Muzzy Petro and hooked by Donna M. Stone, The Hills, Texas, 2017. DREW RICE

David's Vine

I chose to hook the pattern *David's Vine* by Searsport Rug Hooking after seeing it displayed at Sauder Village and reading its entry in *Celebration XXIII*. I met with Chris, the designer of the pattern, as I wanted to make some changes to the original design. My rug was going to be used on the floor, so I didn't want a bird in the pattern. I only wanted to use the center of the original rug pattern, and I also needed the width enlarged so as to be in better balance with the length.

I asked Diane Stoffel, my teacher at the upcoming workshop at St. Joseph's College in Maine, to color plan and supply the wool for this pattern. I arrived at camp to find a packet of materials bearing my name. I started hooking two of the largest motifs using her dip-dyed material. The smaller motifs were hooked with her material, wool I brought, and wool chosen by both of us. We used vibrant, light colors with a dark background. The materials I used includes many dyeing techniques: casserole dye, dip dye, spot dye, over-dye, swatch dye, as-is wool, and recycled wool.

The colors are definitely enhanced by the black background. The background was hooked with three pieces of as-is black wool: solid black recycled skirt, black and gray plaid, and brown-and-black striped wool. I kept balance in the rug by repeating color throughout.

Unexpectedly, I love the background most in this rug. It is hooked in a #6 cut and vibrates with movement without detracting from the design. I drew

S-figures evenly on the background and then used the gray plaid on the "S." Around the S-figures and the motifs in the rug, I hooked a row of solid black. Lastly, I filled the voids with the brown-black striped wool.

I enjoy rug hooking because it has no boundaries and stretches the mind with its endless creativity. I hook different subjects with each pattern I choose. I have hooked geometric, fractur, Orientals, paisley, and original design patterns. I always feel the current rug

I am working on is the best I have ever done. I love the planning and development that goes into a hand-hooked rug. I also love hooking in rug groups. We all become close friends.

> In The Judges' Eyes: *Striking colors move around well against a very dark background; Beautiful color and contrast. Nicely hooked. Pretty background technique.*

Cathryn Williams
Los Gatos, California

Cathryn is a retired librarian. She splits her time between Maine and California and belongs to two ATHA groups: Maine Tin Pedlars and California Peninsula Rugmakers. She is also a McGown Certified Instructor and has led classes in Maine. This is her third appearance in Celebration.

David's Vine, 36" x 72", #3- and 6-cut hand-dyed, recycled, and as-is wool on linen. Designed by Searsport Rug Hooking and hooked by Cathryn Williams, Los Gatos, California, 2017. EVAN TCHELEPI

Home on the Mississippi

Home on the Mississippi was started with the guidance of Gail Walden (McGown Certified Instructor) in 1992 at the Northern McGown Teachers Workshop. After the class, the piece went to the Claire DeRoos class at Chautauqua Rug School for some trees. I didn't have the time necessary at that point to do the piece justice. I needed to observe more examples of finished pictorials and nature. Following a long hiatus away from actively hooking, this piece sat in a storage bin for many years, to be rediscovered and picked up in December 2016. It received my full attention until I finished it about five months later. I did not follow the original color plan of the Currier and Ives illustration that inspired it; I used artistic license and tried to develop an appropriate representation and feeling of the art style. I designed this rug after the McGown Teacher Workshops requested more large, challenging pictorials. I enjoyed completing this piece. The fact that it was completed so many years after it was started allowed me to apply my learning about pictorials over the years to its development and gave me great pleasure in the end result.

The materials included in this rug include Colorama Wool swatches, pieces I dyed for the clouds and sky, and the water is "vintage" wool from Rose Cottage. I have a barrel of wool from Rose Cottage and try to use some in each one of my pieces. I've been doing this for the past ten years or so.

Perhaps the most interesting thing about the development of the piece is the use of Colorama Wool #96 (a swatch with spots), not only for the roof of the house, but also for the Spanish moss that hangs from all of the trees. The repetition of that swatch produces continuity throughout the piece.

I firmly believe that the finishing of a piece can make or break it. So, I invest in professional framing, and once I find a good framer, I tend to use them exclusively. In preparation for framing, I sew a double row around the piece and also press and steam it. I believe it's well worth the effort and expense.

My first project was a 16" geometric pattern, *Stained Glass*, from Pearl K. McGown. In those days, Pearl donated a hook and a pattern to Girl Scout troops who had a qualified teacher to guide them through the project. Most of those in my troop finished the project.

I don't hook for the recognition: I do it because it engages my hands, my mind, and my heart. I love it and the friendships I've made because of this art form.

> In The Judges' Eyes: *Good use of values and colors; More colorful than many Currier and Ives adaptations. The precise technique keeps details crisp; Wonderful use of color and light. Really great detail in the hooking.*

Jane McGown Flynn
Holden, Massachusetts

Jane is a retired designer and businesswoman. She belongs to the National Guild of Pearl K. McGown Hookrafters. She's been hooking for sixty-five years, designing for fifty-five, and treasures every minute. This is her first appearance in Celebration.

Home on the Mississippi, 39" x 24", #3-cut Colorama Wool swatches and hand-dyed wool on burlap. Inspired by a Currier and Ives illustration and designed and hooked by Jane McGown Flynn, Holden, Massachusetts, 2016. JANE MCWHORTER OF BLUE SKY PRODUCTIONS

Les Toutes Fleurs

I purchased this pattern many years ago because I wanted to challenge myself to learn how to hook fine-shaded flowers. It will always be a favorite rug for me because I learned so much from it.

Truthfully, there was nothing too special about my materials. Most anyone would choose swatches for the shading of the flowers. I chose a nine-value swatch for the water lily because the petals touch each other in so many places. I used cording on the edge of the rug (not my usual method), and that did make for a nicely finished edge.

I studied tons of photographs of fine-shaded flower rugs as I was making my color plan. Nearly all of the examples had a very dark background, and the flowers were hooked in their real-life colors. However, that wasn't a color scheme that I wanted in my home, so I hooked all the flowers in shades of red and blue. As a result, this very traditional floral pattern has a sort of updated feel.

I initially imaged the entire background would be cream, but a skilled teacher, Lynne Howard, guided me toward using two background colors. I dyed the cream background in a kettle but did not stir the wool too much as it was dyeing, in order to provide variation in the cream background. I purchased the minty-green background from several different vendors and also dyed some at home. I kept my piles of green separate. Whenever I was cutting green strips, I made sure to cut fabric from each of the piles. This way, the several shades of green were balanced throughout the rug.

The center motif was particularly challenging. I hooked it as drawn and was very pleased that I'd managed to pull off the shading of the water lily.

Then it began to bother me that the lily perspective and the leaf perspective were at different angles. The leaf was drawn as if looking down on the flower, but the lily was drawn as if viewed from the front. So I tore out the leaf, redrew it, and rehooked it. I liked that better, but the motif was no longer centered. Argh! To address this problem, I added butterflies above the lily. While I was at it, I put some light blue squiggles in the background to suggest water and create more movement. At first, I wasn't sure

I totally loved my changes, but I really could not face messing around with it any further. Over time, I've come to like the butterflies very much.

I learned quite a lot about hooking shaded flowers and leaves from this rug. I sought out tips for hooking and binding a round piece so that it stays round. I tried a different binding technique than I'd done in the past, and I liked the result. Most importantly, I learned to be brave about starting a project that I wasn't sure I'd be able to handle.

In The Judges' Eyes: *A clean palette and wonderful work in the background. Simple yet elegant; A quiet floral with good technique. Fetching green background; Nice color plan and shading.*

Heidi Grevstad
Portland, Oregon

Heidi is a registered nurse and certified diabetes educator. Les Toutes Fleurs *won a Best in Division ribbon at the 2017 Oregon State Fair and was exhibited in the "Power of Flowers" show at the Latimer Quilt and Textile Center in May 2018. This is her first appearance in* Celebration.

Les Toutes Fleurs*, 41" round, #3-cut hand-dyed wool on burlap. Designed by Rittermere-Hurst-Field and hooked by Heidi Grevstad, Portland, Oregon, 2017. OWEN CAREY

Scotty McGruff

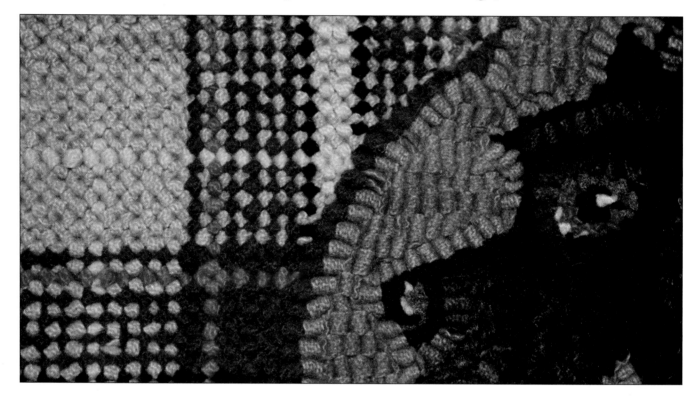

This rug was the subject of a class at WTW (Western Teachers Workshop). The theme of the day was "black animals." Our teacher for this project, Chris Ward, brought lots of books about Scottish plaids. I looked through a book and flagged the plaids that appealed to me. All my favorites had yellow-greens and light blues.

Adding a bit of yellow, orange, and black along with the yellow-green and light blue, I made up my plaid as I hooked the "warp." I decided to add burgundy to the mix to go with the dirty purple background for Scotty. Scotty has such a lively face, and it was fun turning him into a perfect little Scotch terrier, all trimmed up.

Hooking plaid is double hooking, and it has to be exact. This pattern came on rug warp, which is perfectly symmetrical and good for laying out the plaid. In #3 cut, the warp is hooked down, skipping one space between each loop and each row. The weft is then hooked across in the spaces. The weft is harder to hook because the backing is tighter, with half of the loops already in. I had to pace myself and only hook a bit each day.

To finish the rug, I used the "roll forward" technique and whipped with yarns that I collected at yarn shops. I sewed on a sleeve to hold a dowel with eye screws and used fishing wire to hang my rug. I'll probably make a pillow out of this rug when it's done "showing."

My mother hooked and braided rugs all my life. Over the years, hooked rugs became her art form. In 1996, she got an invitation to join a new group, an ATHA chapter called Wine Country Rug Hookers. We decided it was time for me to learn to hook. We enjoyed the WCRH members. WCRH hosted several workshops and expanded our hooking world. When I started teaching in 2003, I learned a lot more from attending rug camps and WTW.

I enjoy rug hooking because I love color! I am excited to create rugs that are pleasing in design, realism, color, and dynamics. I like challenges that take me down a road not visited and seeing how a change in value can fix the color plan. Rug hooking has opened up a world of friends and events. Plus, my mother and I enjoyed sharing many of those adventures together.

In The Judges' Eyes: *Colors in the plaid are in the dog! Look at the eye and fur; One has to admire the incredible precision in this plaid. Bravo; Wonderful technique. Terrific ability to hook a plaid design throughout. All around nice rug.*

Scotty McGruff, 16" x 16", #3- to 5-cut hand-dyed wool on rug warp. Designed by Jane McGown Flynn and hooked by Laura Pierce, Petaluma, California, 2016.

Laura Pierce
Petaluma, California

Laura is a Jill of many trades, working in data processing, delivery, drafting, and tasting room and winery sales. She and her husband have also raised two children. Scotty McGruff *won Best of Show at the 2017 Sonoma County Fair. This is her eighth appearance in* Celebration.

Song of Persia

I love the design of this pattern. I selected it after looking through the thousands of patterns of completed rugs and commentary in "Pearl's Collections," which is a photographic review on CDs of North American hooked rugs from the twentieth century, presented by the National Guild of Pearl K. McGown Hookrafters..

I selected colors that fit in with the colors I have in my home. I used Margaret Howell's special color formulas as well as TOD and Doris Grice formulas. I dyed eight-shade swatches on ¼–½-yard pieces. Since I dye my own wool, I can dye larger-sized swatches and have less waste. I did all my dyeing in pots, which gave me a more even color for this rug.

I originally planned to use the warp from this rug for the fringe after seeing an example that Iris Simpson had hooked at the Green Mountain Rug School, but I quickly learned that didn't work with monk's cloth. Eventually, by chance, I watched a forty-five-second YouTube video on how to repair kilim carpets and learned of a technique that would work. I threaded two strands of the rug warp weft into a crewel needle and pulled it up one side of the kilim stitch and down the other side, pulling it with a pair of pliers. Now, I had monk's cloth fringe joined by rug warp strands. Iris Simpson was my advisor and "sounding board" through this effort. I arrived at her class with all of my wool dyed and planned to select the background color after I got started. Wrong! I learned I needed to select my background first. Stephanie Allen-Krauss of the Green

Mountain Rug School was there to help me select from numerous fabrics and colors. I chose a Dorr dark brown heather #5512, which had hints of blue and red. She warned me of the difficulty in hooking a plaid textured wool in a #3 cut and suggested I try a sample of the washed wool first. I followed her advice but fell in love with the look and colors. It is hard to hook and doesn't look very good on the back, but other than that, it can be hooked in any direction, and the loops do not show. Would I choose it again? Absolutely.

I love every aspect of rug hooking. There's a meditative quality of just pulling the loops. It gives me time to think and

remember. It is rewarding to create a thing of beauty that also has a utilitarian purpose. I love that I will be able to leave heirlooms that are part of me to my children and their children. I look forward to hooking every single day and the challenges it continues to present to me.

In The Judges' Eyes: *The placement of golds throughout adds elegance to a refined design. By crafting the fringe we feel the hands of a maker; Beautiful color plan, shaded nicely, lovely border.*

Lee Williams
Stigler, Oklahoma

Lee is a retired co-owner of a printing and publishing company. She first began rug hooking in 1970 and started up again in 2016 after a hiatus. Her rug Baghdad *won the First Place People's Choice Award at the OK Wool Harvest in 2016. This is her first appearance in* Celebration.

Song of Persia, 36" x 67½", #3-cut hand-dyed and as-is wool on monk's cloth. Designed by Jane McGown Flynn and hooked by Lee Williams, Stigler, Oklahoma, 2017. HUNTER EDWARDS

Tiffany

I have long admired the art of both Claude Monet and Louis Comfort Tiffany and enjoyed my visits to Claude Monet's home and gardens in Giverny, France, and the Tiffany exhibitions at the Metropolitan Museum of Art in New York City. I was delighted to see a completed rug from a commercial pattern of Tiffany's *Magnolias and Irises* in *Rug Hooking* magazine. At that stage of my hooking "career," I never imaged one could hook a stained glass window.

The pattern *Tiffany*, designed by Pearl McGown and Jane McGown Flynn, was offered on monk's cloth by House of Price, now available through Honey Bee Hive. I chose to use Jane Olson's swatches, as those were what the rug hookers in my area were using at the time. I was so inspired by the colors in the original stained glass and at Giverny that I wanted to replicate those colors as closely as possible. I printed several photos of the original stained glass piece and tried my best to use those colors.

My favorite part of the piece is the water, both the stream and the lake, because water illustrates movement and life, just as the irises do. Coincidentally, the "river of life" theme in this Tiffany window is prevalent in Tiffany landscapes created for memorials. This piece was designed as a memorial and was originally installed in a mausoleum in a Brooklyn cemetery.

The biggest lessons learned were not to give up on something and to rely on the expertise of a great teacher. I owe a big thank you to my teacher, Diane Stoffel, without whom I would never have unearthed this project and given it

another try. When I showed this piece to her, she told me I didn't have to take out everything I had hooked fifteen years earlier. I could incorporate smaller cuts. I also learned that using Diane's great over-dyed wools would do much of the work for me. I didn't have to continue to use multiple pieces of wool in the leaves, irises, sky, and water to achieve my desired subtlety of shading.

Rug hooking means many things to me. The challenge of interpreting other media into fiber art inspires me. I have hooked everything from photographs I've taken around the world, to a famous piece of stained glass, to a watercolor painting. The community of rug hooking is equally important to me. I have traveled all over the United States to

rug-hooking classes and workshops, in addition to belonging to several ATHA guilds. I have enjoyed the pleasure of meeting so many great people at these events, some of whom have become close friends. I have found the love, friendship, support, camaraderie, and indeed, family to be the great bonus of this wonderful art of ours.

In The Judges' Eyes: *The light in the sky draws us to the distant water. Consistent variegations are balanced by the lead lines and tree branches; Beautiful vibrant colors. The hooker has achieved the look of stained glass. Very nicely done.*

Susan Naples
Santa Ana, California

Susan is the founder and CEO of a community association management business. Her work has won awards at the Orange County (California) Fair and the Los Angeles County Fair. This is her fifth appearance in Celebration.

Tiffany, 22" x 32", #3- to 5-cut hand-dyed wool on monk's cloth. Designed by Pearl McGown and Jane McGown Flynn and hooked by Susan Naples, Santa Ana, California, 2016.

Tree Study IV

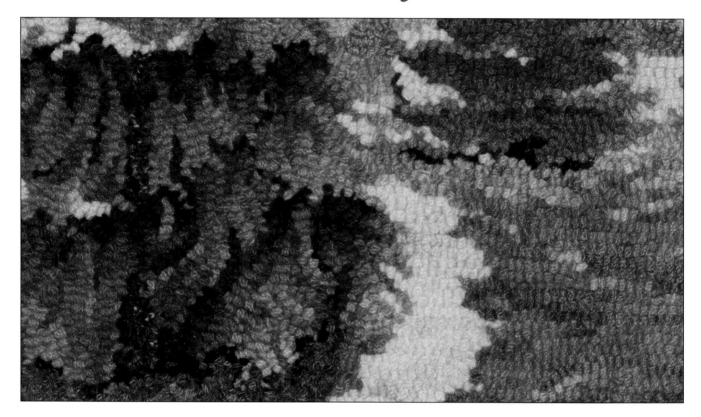

I created this rug to teach the teachers at the Southern McGown Teachers Workshop in October of 2017. It was the last leg of the requirements that I needed to complete to become a McGown Certified Instructor.

My goal was to show depth in the piece and to be able to distinguish one type of tree from the other. I also wanted to make it a winter scene. For the tree in the distance (spruce), I used the least saturated colors of green, the least amount of detail, and the least amount of contrast. This gives the tree the illusion of being further away. For the tree in the middle front (also spruce), I used the most saturated of the tree colors, which then made this tree the focal point. The

eye is drawn to the detail and the more vibrant color. The greatest amount of contrast within the tree gave a feeling of depth within the tree itself. The tree on the left is a balsam tree. The color for that tree was the most challenging to obtain. It is close to the front of the picture, so it needed to be saturated, but it also had to be different enough in hue to distinguish it from the focal-point spruce.

All of the trees were hooked with value swatches. They needed to be different enough to allow the viewer to tell one tree from the other but also pleasant to look at together. I dyed many, many swatches for this rug before I came up with a combination that satisfied me.

I first got into rug hooking when I was at a knit-in (much like a hook-in, except for knitters), and there was a woman hooking (now a close friend, Janet Burg). I spoke with her and told her that I had always wanted to learn how to hook. As luck would have it, she was the president of a local guild and invited me to come check it out. The rest is history. I have always enjoyed needle arts and have done them all my life. What intrigues me about rug hooking is that you can design the piece, dye the wool, and then hook. I like the amount of control you have over making a piece your own work of art. And, as many will agree, the rhythm of pulling loops is very soothing to the nerves.

In The Judges' Eyes: *Sky is wonderful; Beautiful moody sky behind the trees in winter, foreground, mid-ground and background beautifully executed. Bravo; Good study to share with other rug hookers; Nice detail and painted winter sky.*

Deb Szwed
Taylor, Michigan

Deb is a retired project management professional and has started teaching rug hooking. She is the treasurer of the Southern McGown Teachers Workshop and has written articles for Rug Hooking *magazine and the McGown newsletter. This is her second appearance in* Celebration.

Tree Study IV, 14¾" x 16½", #3- and 4-cut wool on linen. Designed by Linda Powell and hooked by Deb Szwed, Taylor, Michigan, 2017. JOHN ANGUS

Victoria Avenue

I'm a real estate agent and always on the lookout for patterns with houses. The main reason this appealed to me, however, is because I used to own and live in a large, historic Victorian home from 1905. The home on the far left side of the rug was very similar to mine in style, so I used the old color scheme of my home when color planning.

Ingrid Hieronimus designed the pattern, and I want to give a special shout-out to my teacher, Nancy Terhar, who helped me get started on this project. Even though the pattern is fairly large, I decided to use a #3 cut in order to capture the fine details in the homes, trees, and especially, the fencing, patterned after my great-grandmother Kate's iron cemetery fencing. I also used a #4 and a bit of #6 in the clouds and sky to make the storm seem more ominous.

Pictures of this rug, hooked as a summer scene, were supplied with the pattern—green trees, flowers, beautiful blue sky, etc. I wanted more emotion and mystery in my rug, though, so I decided to explore an autumn theme with stormy skies. It's also my favorite season of the year! I dyed a number of colors for the trees and dyed a large quantity for the sky. I also used a lot of wool from my stash, which was hand-dyed by various teachers. The tumultuous clouds were particularly difficult to do, mainly struggling to get the right contrast and contours.

I love the little details I added to the pattern. My four-year-old grandson wanted crows in the sky and pumpkins on the porch. I decided the colorful autumn leaves

Katy Powell
Milwaukie, Oregon

Katy is a real estate broker. She belongs to ATHA Region 11. She's also been involved with other craft projects, such as quilting, cross-stitch, crocheting, knitting, and appliqué. This is her third appearance in Celebration.

on the ground and my great-grandmother's cemetery fence would be perfect for capturing the mood of the piece.

I first got started in rug hooking when I worked for my father's punch hooking company, Rumplestiltskins, back in the '70s. He advertised his electric punch needle in *Rug Hooking* magazine, and I became fascinated with the beautiful and artistic hand-hooked rugs. It wasn't until years later that I went to my first rug camp, Friends by the Sea, in Rockaway, Oregon, in 2001. I've been hooking ever since!

In The Judges' Eyes: *The dark clouds add drama to the staid design. Good choices of values and color changes for the trees, the lighter shades help define the red and blue houses; Crisp, with stylized trees and a great fall sky. It is nice that not every house has their pumpkins out. Iron fencing is well done and unifies the avenue.*

Victoria Avenue, 60" x 20", #3- and 4-cut hand-dyed wool on monk's cloth. Designed by Ingrid Hieronimus and hooked by Katy Powell, Milwaukie, Oregon, 2016. OWEN CAREY

Victory Rose

A few years ago, my teacher, Peg Hannum, was retiring and downsizing and was selling her old rug patterns. I didn't need another, so I closed my eyes and didn't look. My friend Patti agreed to take this pattern for *Victory Rose*. Months later, Patti decided to sell "Rose," and another friend, Mary, said she would take it. Needless to say, a few months later, Mary was looking to pass on "Rose." She asked me if I wanted it. I did, but I didn't want to buy another pattern, so Mary gave her to me. Right away, I started color planning and, thanks to Peggy, dyeing my own wool. I use only Woolrich wool in a #3 cut.

First, I spot-dyed the background a mottled black, then tackled the big rose in the center. I dyed two different sets of swatches and cross-swatched them for the big rose, which I was happy with. For the pansy, I used the red from one of the smaller roses and added J.T. 23 to it, which worked fine. This is one of those rugs that seemed to evolve as I started to hook. The large rose in the center was first, and all the others just fell into place. The poppies, however, were particularly challenging. You need to get the depth done right, so you know you're looking into the throat of the flower. Getting those darker values in there gives you the depth.

It took me about ten months to complete, whip around, and press. I entered "Rose" in the Maryland State Fair this summer, where she won first place and judges' choice. So that's the story of *Victory Rose*. Peg, Patti, and Mary can visit any time they would like to.

In The Judges' Eyes: *What can be said other than exquisite, from dye pot to the final loop. The back tells a story of meticulous attention to creating the motifs; The straight-line rug hooking is very effective with all the curvy lines. Bravo; Beautiful workmanship. I think of rugs like this as "a rug of a lifetime," a culmination of talent and technique.*

Marion Sachs
York, Pennsylvania

Marion belongs to the Pearl McGown Conestoga Guild and Woolwrights ATHA group in Lancaster, PA. Aside from rug hooking, she's quilted for twenty years and does needlepoint. This is her sixth appearance in Celebration.

Victory Rose, 60" x 60", #3-cut hand-dyed wool on monk's cloth. Designed by Skaket from Heirloom Rugs and hooked by Marion Sachs, York, Pennsylvania, 2017. BILL BISHOP, IMPACT XPOZURES

Wedgewood Platter

Heirloom Patterns are older patterns, which date to the Pearl McGown era. The current owner of the patterns has not been printing them for almost a decade. I have long collected these patterns, and when I retired from teaching rug hooking three years ago, I sold all but the ones I wanted to hook to my students as a fundraiser for a Palestinian school in Bethlehem.

My husband and I both retired in our early 60s to accept the positions of Liaisons to Israel/Palestine, representing the United Methodist Church. We worked mostly in the West Bank and Gaza, partnering with Christian, Jewish, and Muslim projects working for peace with justice.

Having retired again, this time to Lancaster, Pennsylvania, I completed my McGown certification and taught rug hooking for seventeen years. Three years ago, I retired for the third time! I should say I have much more time to hook, but somehow, the days seem shorter. Anyway, *Wedgewood Platter* is finally complete, and I'm almost finished with another Heirloom Pattern: *Geranium Oval*.

I dyed all eight-value swatches and a spot dye for this rug. I love red! Pomegranates are red, and with a little research, I found that the bush's flowers are red as well. What more could I want! I was going to Maryland Shores Rug School with Nancy Blood, who has been teacher, friend, and mentor for years. I asked Nancy to plan the rug using red and some of the newer bright greens. As usual, Nancy worked her magic

and sent me the formulas to dye, and she laid out the colors.

I began with the pomegranate, of course. However, the pattern was drawn as a large oval with several huge seeds. After hooking, rehooking, and rethinking (all euphemisms for ripping out!), I finally, after a full day's work, produced a decent-looking pom.

My friend Lyn Lovell and I, partners in crime, were avid knitters and sewers. Living in Massachusetts where, at the time, there were dozens of woolen and yarn mills, we managed to squirrel away bags of mill ends for enough projects to last a lifetime. One day, she said she had something new to show me, called rug hooking. I inwardly vowed not to be lured into another fiber arena! Our families were on a ski trip to New

Hampshire, and Lyn suggested she and I visit Dorr Mill where, to please Lyn, I picked up a doorstop kit, replete with hook, a little pattern, and pre-cut hook-by-number strips. The rest is history! I enjoy rug hooking because I find it meditative, and I also had a 200-year-old house with wide pine floors that needed rugs! Other houses later, I find the hooked rugs fit any décor.

> In The Judges' Eyes: *A warm palette and the reds move our eye around; Coloration and shapes are well done; Colors glow and take one's breath away. Beautiful background to boot; Beautiful rich color, fabulous background.*

Peggy Hannum
Lancaster, Pennsylvania

Peggy is a retired high school English teacher and a retired rug hooking teacher. She is a juried member of the Pennsylvania Guild of Craftsmen and has won many awards in their annual guild craft show. This is her tenth appearance in Celebration.

Wedgewood Platter, 27" x 38", #3- and 4-cut hand-dyed wool on linen. Designed by Louise Zeiser of Heirloom Patterns and hooked by Peggy Hannum, Lancaster, Pennsylvania, 2016. BILL BISHOP, IMPACT XPOZURES

Air Traffic Control

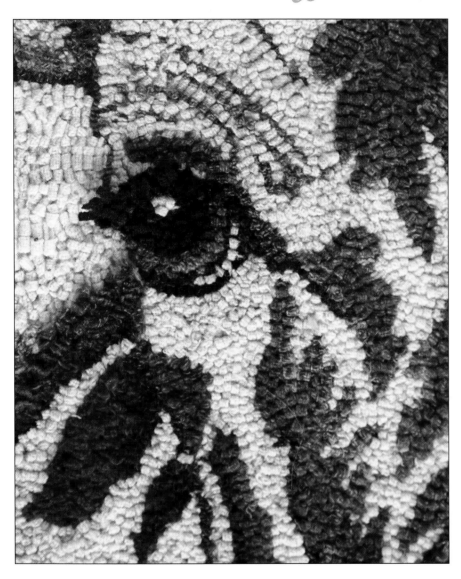

factors when creating a rug. In this rug, my challenge was not only to create the colors of the giraffe but also to capture the dramatic sky behind the animal. To create the giraffe, I used colors from rust tones to oatmeal tones and abrashed over natural wool, using different values to create shadowing to give a realistic look and harmony.

I also used a technique called pixelating, which is raising up the wool two pieces at a time to give dimension to the work. You can choose to cut these pieces or leave them in the loop; for this piece, I chose to cut them. This technique gave me dimension in the giraffe's mane, eyelashes, and head.

To create a realistic picture, there should be subtle differences in the animals. For instance, the eyes are a little different from each other with my rug. As in nature, no animal's face is perfectly symmetrical, so by creating subtle differences in the eyes, you end up with a more natural-looking animal with character and personality, thereby eliminating the stuffed animal look in your rug. I enjoy hooking animals and love any challenge they bring.

I first got started with rug hooking when a friend showed me the rug she had made. I loved it! I enjoy rug hooking because I find it relaxing. It's a wonderful way to express my creativity as well as keep in touch with all of my hooking friends. I have enjoyed a variety of art media throughout my life. Once rug hooking was introduced to me in the year 2000, it captivated me, and I treasure and enjoy it to this day.

The artist Vicki Sawyer creates whimsical looks to her paintings of animals. She continues with her creative sense of humor when she names them, as seen here in her painting of a giraffe with a bird on its head called *Air Traffic Control*.

Color is one of the most important

Anne Bond
Northville, Michigan

Anne has been a salon and spa owner for thirty years and cosmetologist for over forty years. She's also worked with watercolor, oil painting, drawing, sculpting, lead glass, pottery, and quilting. This is her fourth appearance in Celebration.

Air Traffic Control, 26" x 36", #3- to 5-cut hand-dyed wool on linen. Adapted with permission from a painting by Vicki Sawyer and designed and hooked by Anne Bond, Northville, Michigan, 2017. MERIDETH PETERSON

Beautiful Angel

For my Rock River Rug Retreat a few years ago, I searched and selected a vintage Christmas postcard, which had a lovely face that I could develop under the tutelage of Tish Murphy. To enlarge the printout, I graphed the image and linen backing in proportion to fit the needed dimensions of my frame. I wanted this piece to incorporate only 100% wool, and my thirty-five-year stockpile of "noodles" supplied the wool for the face, arms, and clouds, leaving very little dent in my stash.

All of the colors I selected were based on the postcard image I printed from the computer. I only had to dye the sky outside of my stockpile, which came from two dye formulas by Pris Butler, which were almost identical in hue but slightly different in value. Dyeing the sky was a simple open-pan method with very little stirring, to attain a mottled effect.

That nose was such a struggle! It refused to come together for over a day and a half and would have taken even longer if not for Tish Murphy's talented assistance. She had just the right "threads" of grays, browns, and textures—which she carries around in her pocket—that were just what we needed to get the subtle shadows needed for the final product.

It was so amazing to see how the adage "color gets all the credit while value does the work" really is true. Having achieved the execution of the lovely face, I've gained the knowledge I sought to potentially be able to work with a student who selects a similar design.

I first got started in rug hooking in the summer of 1980. A friend and I

were enjoying a music event at a band shell in a park in Eau Claire, Wisconsin, when we saw these "older" ladies making what we thought were quilts. To our surprise, they were rugs, and the techniques they used were like nothing I had ever done before. I added my name to their list of potential students

and took my first hook to hand the following January in 1981. When it comes to rug hooking, I think I love the color the most, as well as the feel of the wool; it's the same in my other favorite pastime, knitting. I also enjoy the satisfaction of seeing the vision take shape of what I want my piece to be.

In The Judges' Eyes: *Dreamy face; The angel is indeed beautifully worked. A precious face and her hair just glows; Beautiful skin tones and hair.*

Beautiful Angel, 24" x 18", #3- and 4-cut hand-dyed wool on linen. Adapted from a vintage postcard titled "Christmas Postcard No. 8286" from Raphael Tuck & Sons, circa 1908, and designed and hooked by Patty Piek-Groth, Janesville, Wisconsin, 2017.

Patty Piek-Groth
Janesville, Wisconsin

Patty is a retired public special education teacher. She's presently a teacher for the Decorah Rug School in Decorah, Iowa. Beautiful Angel *has won first place at the Heart of Wisconsin September guild hook-in and was on exhibit at the Rock River Rug Retreat in October 2017. This is her first appearance in* Celebration.

Christmas Postcard

As a long-time antique collector, I'm always looking for something different in a pattern, something primitive that I can relate to and use in our rustic cabin. While looking through our album of old postcards, I came upon the collection of old German Santa cards. Many showed Santa in a green or brown suit, but this one stood out among all the others, even though Santa wore red! Like most German postcards, the colors were clear and vivid. This postcard had a 1912 postmark, and the picture had an Old-World feel with just the right amount of detail in the background—not too simple and not too cluttered. I had found my next rug-hooking challenge!

Other than the bright red background, which is as-is wool, the rug is overdyed. My real concern came with Santa's beard and mustache; they both needed texture. My friend Jan gave me some wool yarn, which I hooked flowing recklessly like hair over the darker tones in the already hooked beard. It took a while, using lots of yarn, before getting the desired texture and feel with a three-dimensional look. The mustache needed another layering, which was accomplished with needle felting and wool roving.

My valued workshop instructor, Gene Shepherd, and I agreed that the challenge would be hooking Santa's eyes. Following Gene's advice, I hooked and rehooked the eyes. Once they took on a life of their own, I felt satisfied. To me, that accomplishment was key in making this rug "good" versus "okay." Among some of the toys that Santa carried in the postcard were a rifle and a whip. Now this was probably normal in 1912, but not in today's society. I also considered the questioning looks I'd get from our grandchildren! Using my artistic license, I changed the rifle and whip to a large candy cane. I felt that this change worked and also added a bit of color to a somewhat drab area.

I had been a long-time admirer of hooked rugs, especially high-priced primitive ones found at antique shows that were unaffordable to me. I knew about an excellent rug-hooking teacher in the area, the dear, notable Jean White. A month after my retirement in 2004, I took three lessons from Jean and was hooked. Rug hooking gives me a sense of accomplishment and pride. It also satisfies the need for fellowship with like-minded friends, whether hooking, sharing information, or just visiting. All these things together make me happy!

Donna Tackett
Nashville, Indiana

Donna is happily retired after a long career as a senior executive assistant. Christmas Postcard *won first place at the 2016 Indiana State Fair rug hooking competition. This is her first appearance in* Celebration.

In The Judges' Eyes: *The face and adding roving for dimension brings our attention to Santa; Lovely holiday rug; nice use of complementary colors and detail.*

Christmas Postcard, 36" x 24", #3- to 7-cut hand-dyed and as-is wool and wool yarn on linen. Adapted from an antique postcard and designed and hooked by Donna Tackett, Nashville, Indiana, 2016. DEBBIE DUNBAR

Early Light

In an issue of *Nature Conservancy Magazine*, I saw an article with photographs of Adirondack Park in New York State. The pictures were all beautiful, but there was one that took my breath away. It wasn't so much the subject matter—a man and his dog on a lake in the early morning—but the effect of the hazy light. I knew immediately that I wanted to try to capture that emotion in a hooked-rug piece.

I sent the magazine photograph to Marjorie Duizer, with whom I would be studying at Ohio Rug Camp at Punderson Manor Resort. She felt it was a picture that could be hooked, and she custom-dyed the wool for me. The sky and water dictated the color; it had to be monochromatic with many, many values. She captured the mood of the photograph beautifully.

The biggest challenge for me was trying to translate the different effects of light on the water and sky. As I worked small sections, I kept standing back from the canvas to see whether the effect of the hooked area seemed consistent with the direction of the imagined light source. I did a considerable amount of "reverse hooking" throughout the rug since my first (and often second) instincts were wrong!

Since I haven't had art training, this rug gave me a greater appreciation for the nuances of color in nature. For me, no sky will ever again be just a blue sky, or just water without shadow and depth. I discovered that small changes in color value can have powerful effects. I also learned that while working on a detailed canvas, it is critical to regularly view it from a distance. The whole really is greater (and truer) than a sum of the parts!

I was first introduced to rug hooking when a friend, Christine Goyer, took me along to her rug hooking group that met at the home of a wonderful local rug hooking mentor to many, Kay Rautenberg. I had no idea what rug hooking was. I bought a small pattern from Kay that morning, and she lent me all the rest: a frame, hook, and wool; she even cut the strips for me. She continued to lend a helpful hand that morning as I made mistake after mistake! By the end of our visit, I was hooked and have been hooking ever since. Although I'm not an artist, rug hooking gives me a sense of what it must be like to paint. I love working in two dimensions to create an image that looks three-dimensional. I love the color, the shading, and the detail. Frankly, it feels magical.

Tena Tarler Rosner
Shaker Heights, Ohio

Tena has a doctorate in Human Development and worked for many years as the Associate Director for Research Administration at Case Western Reserve University's Comprehensive Cancer Center. She is now retired. Early Light *appeared in the rug show at the ATHA biennial in Cleveland in September 2017. This is her first appearance in* Celebration.

Early Light, 17¼" x 11½", #3-cut wool on rug warp. Adapted with permission from a photo by Blake Gordon and designed and hooked by Tena Tarler Rosner, Shaker Heights, Ohio, 2017. SHAKER HEIGHTS MOTO PHOTO

Evan and His Lamb, Luna

I saw a photo of a boy and his lamb in a small newspaper in a nearby town and I recognized that the boy in the black-and-white photo was my neighbor! The story was so heartwarming that I decided to make this rug for Evan. The article mentioned that this photo was taken while Evan and Luna were waiting a long, long time in line to have the lamb judged at our local fair. Luna fell asleep with his head in Evan's hand. The contestants had to train their lambs to lead by hand only, with no collars or ropes. Evan was the last in the long line.

The picture in the newspaper was black and white, so I just used the colors that I thought were the colors of each item. I knew that Evan had a blue plaid shirt, so that was how I decided to hook it. I love Evan's face the most. It hooked so easily, and when I show the rug to anyone, they immediately recognize him. This rug went together so well that I can't say that anything was difficult to hook. I did, however, have to add some darker color to Luna's back because it was quite indistinguishable at first. It faded into the background, so I simply added darker colors.

I didn't have any black wool yarn at home and didn't want to make a trip to town, so I used some dark gray acrylic wool yarn that I had at home to whip the edges. It blended well; however, it did have quite long, fuzzy threads. After the Sauder Village show, I will remove the fuzzy threads, add a black binding, and replace the whipped edge with black wool yarn. It will make the edges stiffer, which will help it hang well.

I was always in awe of anything wool, and the design and colors of hooked-rugs attracted me to a new rug-hooking class in town. I quickly signed up, made a few small items, and bought all the necessary and expensive tools. Then I quit hooking for seventeen years. When I picked it out of the storage trunk later, I fell in love with hooking all over again.

In The Judges' Eyes: *The relationship is endearing without the subjects having eye contact; The plaid shirt was not the easiest choice but likely the very best. All eyes on Evan; Very nice shading and detail on Evan.*

Marilyn Becker
Wausau, Wisconsin

Marilyn is retired and, aside from rug hooking, loves hand quilting, knitting, crocheting, embroidery, hardanger, and other stitching. Her rugs have been shown in Sauder Village and at the Wisconsin Museum of Quilts and Fiber Arts. This is her fifth appearance in Celebration.

Evan and His Lamb, Luna, 23" x 32", #3- and 4-cut hand-dyed wool and acrylic yarn binding on cotton rug warp. Adapted with permission from a photo found in the Record Review in *The Tribune Phonograph* and designed and hooked by Marilyn Becker, Wausau, Wisconsin, 2016.

Happy Man

When I discovered the image of *Happy Man*, I was intrigued by the expression and character of his face and the pure joy in his smile. I kept studying the face and trying to figure out how I could possibly reproduce these expressions and feelings with wool yarn. The original artist of the painting lives in India, and I managed to contact him after a bit of trial and error. He was very gracious and gave me permission to adapt his painting and even sent me a high-resolution image so I could get the colors and details just right. Then I was all set.

I started by determining the size that I wanted for the final rug, then, once the outside dimensions were drawn, I drew *Happy Man*. The backing material I used is very fine, so the yarns I used had to either be very fine or else I had to unravel thicker yarns to one or two strands. As always, finding the correct colors was a real challenge. One of these days, I'm going to try dyeing my own yarn! I started by hooking the lips, and I must say, they looked really funny at first. Everyone who saw this rug in the beginning stages said, "Oh, I don't know about this one." But I persisted because in my head, I could just "see" the final product.

The wrinkles, folds, and creases of his face, as well as his whiskers, were really challenging, and there are lots of areas that I hooked, pulled out, hooked, pulled out. . . When *Happy Man* was finished, I did the background with a dark gray wool roving that I had "unraveled." But it just wasn't right, so I pulled it all out and spent hours at a local wool shop trying to find the right color and texture. To date, *Happy Man* is the most challenging rug I have hooked.

I started rug hooking in 2010 after seeing an exhibition. I was looking for a new fiber-art challenge and could see the limitless possibilities with this art form. I love rug hooking because it is wonderfully relaxing, but at the same time, I find it artistically challenging. I have always been involved in fiber art in one form or another. When I was working, it was usually as a "de-stressing" mechanism, but now it is pure pleasure!

In The Judges' Eyes: *Palette adds to the peaceful features; Color is stunning and technique precise; Nice shading in the face.*

Susan Baker
Stanbridge East, Quebec, Canada

Susan is a retired research scientist in drug metabolism and pharmacokinetics. Following retirement, she moved to the country and now spends her time helping to feed the homeless and needy and working in her studio on various fiber art projects. This is her third appearance in Celebration.

Happy Man, 20" x 15½", wool yarn on unidentified fabric (400 holes per square inch, likely cotton). Adapted with permission from a painting by Rajasekharan Parameswaran, and designed and hooked by Susan Baker, Stanbridge East, Quebec, Canada, 2017. TONY PEIRCE

Home of Jesse Smith in 1847

When I started thinking about creating this rug, I knew two things. One, I wanted Leonard Feenan to create the pattern for me, and two, I wanted to hook it in all sepia-valued wool, both as a nod to the original black and white photo I worked from and to give the piece an aged, historical feel. I loved creating this rug and gifting it to my dear friends, Penny Honetor and her husband, Rob Glazier. I surprised them on New Year's Eve 2016 with the finished rug.

I definitely feel using only hand-dyed sepia wool in a ten-value spectrum enhanced the historical feel of the piece. The majority of the wool was dyed over Dorr natural. A small houndstooth textured wool was overdyed in every other value and used primarily in the cobblestones and ground.

I love how the bushes in front of the house turned out. I may have a stronger feeling for them because I wasn't sure how to approach them, and my wonderful instructor, Joyce Krueger, was able to give me some pointers. I also really like how the sky developed into a winter sky. It was especially important to me that the sky lighten as it neared the house and trees, or I would visually lose these items. This was one challenge I faced working exclusively in one color; there needed to be enough value change throughout the piece to help the viewer see the detail clearly.

Oddly, this rug seemed to fight me the entire way. Or maybe I had a relatively low expectation on its difficulty. The first challenge was that the original photo was from 1847 and was very grainy, so I had to research a lot to fill in the detail. Some parts of the picture were just too dark, and I had to visually lighten them and guess how they would look. The porch was a challenge as well. I rehooked the pillars about five times because they didn't come out right. I needed the shading to change by two to three values to distinguish them as square pillars, but they kept getting distorted.

I learned so much about working in a monochromatic scheme with this rug. In a colored piece, you can rely a lot on the color to explain the details to the viewer, but in a monochromatic rug such as this, I feel the artist has to work extra hard to communicate the detail. The placement of the values is crucial to add to the piece, and care needs to be taken to not place values of different objects too close together, or the image and detail can become completely lost. I just know this rug wouldn't be the same if hooked in color.

In The Judges' Eyes: *To depict the subject in sepia pays homage to the period and story. Look closely at any section and observe the artistic selection of just the right texture; Excellent monochromatic rug. Great perspective detail and hooking technique.*

Mary McGrath
Mukwonago, Wisconsin

Mary is a safety coordinator and co-owner of a commercial heating, ventilating, cooling, and refrigeration company in Waukesha, Wisconsin. Home of Jesse Smith in 1847 *was chosen as a People's Choice Award winner at the 2017 Cream City Hook In. This is Mary's fifth appearance in* Celebration.

Home of Jesse Smith in 1847, 38½" x 25½", #3-cut hand-dyed wool on rug warp. Adapted from an image from the Wisconsin Historical Society Image ID: 37928, designed by Leonard Feenan and hooked by Mary McGrath, Mukwonago, Wisconsin, 2016.

King

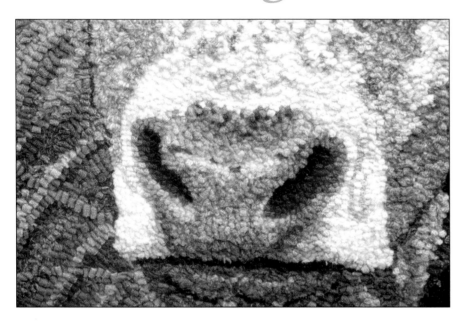

When I saw the photo that inspired this rug, it reminded me of growing up on a farm in Iowa where my father raised Hereford cows. My brother joined 4-H at the age of nine, and King, a Hereford steer, was his project. For a year, he fed, groomed, and trained him. After showing King at the county fair, King was sold. It was a sad day for a nine-year-old and the rest of the family, but it was also an experience in growing up.

The eyelashes are four-ply cotton thread. The ends were pulled through the monk's cloth, knotted at the base, and separated to create a fuller look. To keep the eyelashes in place, they were sprayed with hair spray. I didn't do any special dyeing for this piece. I found all the colors in my stash.

The most challenging area to hook was the bridge of the nose and forehead. The hair grows in a swirl. (He has a cowlick!) All the hair had to be hooked in curves—no straight lines. In order to create that look, the wool colors and values needed to have great contrast.

To finish the piece, I hand-stitched wool on the edges of the hooked piece the same color as on the hooked part. Then I mounted it on stretcher bars. The name of the piece and other information is machine stitched on dark brown wool and hand stitched around the edges on the back. There is also a pocket, machine stitched, on the back that contains the information regarding who took the photo and the copyright.

I started to hook rugs with an interest group in Waukesha, Wisconsin. Then I started to go to rug camps and workshops, including the McGown Teachers Workshop. I enjoy rug hooking because it is an art that can be adapted from almost any type of needlework, painting, etc. There is always a new challenge in each hooked piece you create.

In The Judges' Eyes: *The eyelashes and loops on snout are reasons to see this in person; Stylized grasses echo the curve of the Hereford's red hair; Wonderful lifelike expression.*

King, 19½" x 14½", #3-cut hand-dyed and as-is wool, cotton thread, and natural wool yarn on monk's cloth. Adapted from a photo by James Wheeler and hooked by Joyce Krueger, Waukesha, Wisconsin, 2017.
ART'S CAMERA PLUS

Joyce Krueger
Waukesha, Wisconsin

Joyce is a retired secretary and is also a wife, mother, rug hooker, and rug hooking teacher. She also braids rugs, knits, embroiders, and does counted cross-stitch. She belongs to the Cream City Rug Hooking Guild, the Greater Midwest Teachers Guild, the McGown Guild, and ATHA. This is her fourth appearance in Celebration.

Mac in the Daisies

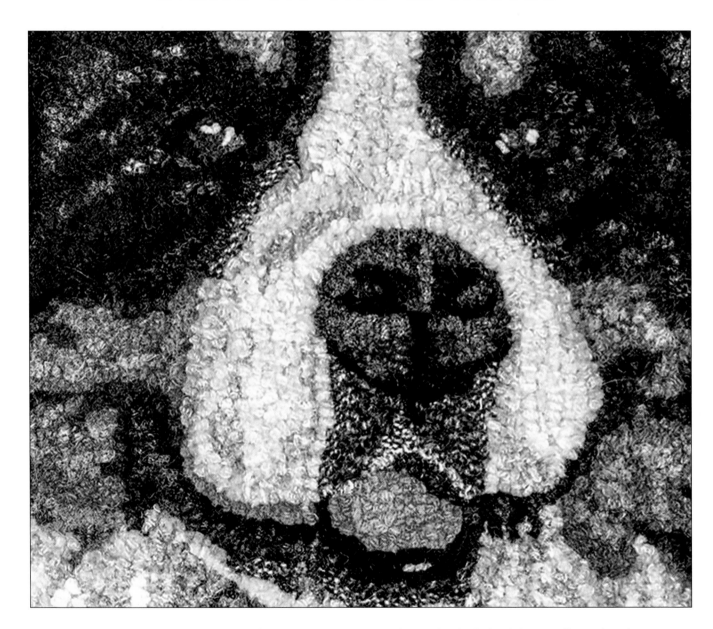

Mac was my heart dog, and he was featured in calendars, magazines, and other dog-related items. He was an AKC champion, obedience, draft, and therapy dog. I waited many years to hook him until I felt my skill matched my wish to honor him and do him well.

For several years, I collected many textures and dyed pieces to accurately portray the black, white, and rust colors of a Bernese Mountain Dog. The many colors of a black dog are very challenging, and collecting the right wool was essential to creating the realistic dog. The background was dyed by Michele Micarelli. She used an approved photograph I

provided, and I think she did an excellent job. Whipping wool was dyed at the same time as the background wool. Mixing the gray and greens was a challenge to keep things looking random and not repetitive when finishing the rug.

I am committed to Bernese Mountain Dogs and compete in conformation, obedience, and draft events. All of my dogs are registered therapy dogs, and I breed them occasionally. I enjoy the social aspects of hooking groups and the challenge of accurately portraying them. My dogs are my passion, and being able to accurately portray them in my rugs is an ongoing challenge. With each one, I feel I am doing a better job.

Mac in the Daisies, 23" x 22", #4-cut hand-dyed and as-is textured wool on rug warp. Adapted from a photograph by "Close Encounters of the Furry Kind" and designed and hooked by Barbie Beck-Wilczek, Littleton, New Hampshire, 2017. ANNE-MARIE LITTENBERG

Barbie Beck-Wilczek
Littleton, New Hampshire

Barbie is retired from a career in the electric utility industry. She belongs to the Green Mountain and Northeast Kingdom in Vermont and Hunterdon County Rug Artisans Guild in New Jersey. This is her third appearance in Celebration.

Maritime Christmas

I saw this pattern online at Encompassing Designs Rug Hooking Studio after some friends of mine visited the studio on a trip to Canada, where they shared a rug I had designed and hooked for them of their Portuguese Water Dogs. The owner of the studio posted a picture of my friends with their rug on her studio's Facebook page. After investigating the Facebook page, I went to Encompassing Design's website and immediately fell in love with this pattern. Since my husband and I are active with our Portuguese Water Dogs in water work, the nautical Christmas theme really appealed to me. I added my dogs to the design, a rope border, and a few dog toys in the doryman's net, and *voilà!*

I tried to use realistic colors and textured wool to emulate the natural texture of the elements. I liked the texture of the bolt wool for the dogs, decking, and sky, and the vibrancy of the hand-dyed wool for the doryman's hat and coat and how it could be used for shading in the coat, hat, and face. Wool yarn added extra texture and shading for the dogs and doryman's beard. Lastly, I couldn't figure out how I was going to hook the netting and fishing line into the piece. I'm not a fan of #3 cuts, so I added cording and netting when the hooking was finished, and I love the effect.

Choosing the colors for the dog toys in the net was challenging. I had to get enough contrasting colors and values. Also, I didn't have the proper hand-dyed wool to effectively hook the boat in the original design. It had to be shaded to look like it was pulled into the dock at an angle, and I couldn't achieve that

effect, so I just redrew the boat from a simple side view. To finish the rug, I rolled the edges over cording and whipped with wool.

I first got started in rug hooking after a friend of mine learned about it and got involved with our local guild, the Crescent Lane Rug Hooking Guild. She showed me a piece she had completed, and I loved it. I went with her to one of

the guild's Monday hook-ins and fell in love with the craft and the people. I've always done some type of needlework, crewel, cross-stitch, knitting, crochet, a little sewing, etc., so this was right up my alley. I love the satisfaction I get from the creative process, and I just love the feel, look, and qualities of wool. I also love a practical and useful piece of art!

In The Judges' Eyes: *The dark lines draw our attention to the face and sage charm; Hooked rope around the edge is nicely done and the perfect frame; Nice design. Good detail and shading in the rope.*

Maritime Christmas, 23½" x 24½", #3- to 6-cut hand-dyed and as-is wool, wool yarn, cording, and netting on linen. Adapted by Angie Myers from a design by Encompassing Designs Rug Hooking Studio and hooked by Donna Culp, Athens, Georgia, 2017.

Donna Culp
Athens, Georgia

Donna is a retired first-grade teacher who took up rug hooking about fifteen years ago. She is very involved with her two Portuguese Water Dogs, participating in activities like water work and agility. This is her first appearance in Celebration.

Orchard House Welcome

I have always admired and appreciated antique textiles and figures, and fancy jacquard coverlets are among my favorites. As a weaver, I can only weave geometric coverlets on my loom, so I enjoy adapting and translating the intricate motifs from the jacquard coverlets to use in my rug hooking. The house and tree border used by the Gilmour Brothers (circa 1839) was the perfect choice for a welcome rug.

The inspiration for the colors of this rug comes from colors traditionally used in antique coverlets: indigo, madder, and natural cotton or linen. Most of the time when you see this motif, it is done in two colors, but I wanted this to be different, so I decided to add an additional color. I selected a deep blue/black texture with a small, multi-colored plaid for the indigo background, dyed an aged natural, and added a pink with brown overtones to resemble faded aged madder, which was an early red dye. I dyed over Dorr natural wool using an open-pan mottled dye method.

The most challenging part of the rug was hooking the trees. Before I did any hooking on this rug, I drew guidelines on the linen every two inches to have a reference point, in case I needed help to keep the color pattern in order and the lines straight. I'm so glad that I did! I was initially going to hook one tree at a time, but not too far into hooking the first tree, I decided that it would be better to work on them simultaneously, and that would allow me to have them be closer to mirror images. I worked

a few rows on one and then went over to hook on the other side and hooked the same on the second tree, counting loops and spaces in the linen to match the first one, all the while making sure I was keeping the rows of color in the correct row of linen. I found that I couldn't hook any of the background in until the trees were completed because it was too difficult for me to count and maintain the order and spacing. I was really glad when this part of the rug was finished!

I have always felt an attraction to antique textiles, their history, and the processes by which they were made. I think it is important to keep these traditions alive and to pass them on, so they aren't lost or forgotten. I enjoy the process of working on a rug from start to finish: designing patterns, choosing colors, dyeing wool, and seeing the rug to completion. The greatest enjoyment, though, comes from the strong friendships and the bonds that I have with my other hooking friends. There has been a lot of laughter, tears, and problems solved at hooking get-togethers!

Diane Gill
Martinsburg, West Virginia

Diane is a homemaker, wife, mother, and grandmother of three. She also has an Etsy store, DyeanneG, where she offers patterns and hand-dyed wool. She's a member of two ATHA guilds: With Hands and Hearts Antietam Fiber Artists and Goose Creek Ruggers. This is her second appearance in Celebration.

Orchard House Welcome, 40½" x 21", #4- and 8-cut wool on linen. Adapted from a coverlet border pattern by the Gilmour Brothers and designed and hooked by Diane Gill, Martinsburg, West Virginia, 2017. KELLY HAHN PHOTOGRAPHY

Springtime on the Island from Grammy's Back Door

I was inspired to create this rug from happy memories of rowing with my brother and our dog from the family cottage in Maine. I chose a red and green split complementary color plan for balance and an extremely limited palette for the most harmony. I added a ceramic butterfly and did a beaded butterfly for a greater contrast of texture.

I positively loved working as much pearlescent sheen as possible into the largest flower, stuffing it in a 3-D fashion through trapunto. Maintaining perspective through color intensity and value required a very large selection of wools, which was a challenge to work through.

After reading several books on advice by artists, I really pushed my boundaries through shading and pearlescent sheen together and love how much closer to nature the results are. To finish the rug, I curled and whipped the edges with tightly spun sport-weight wool yarn.

I got started rug hooking at our local YWCA in a craft class by Ruth Hall, who was born in the 1800s, and learned to hook as they did back then, not as we do now. I love rug hooking because the concentration it requires takes me from the realities of this world to a place of peace. I knit, crochet, quilt, and embroider but never drew a thing in my life until I retired and drew my first rug—a life-changing experience.

Springtime on the Island from Grammy's Back Door, 30" x 30", #3-cut hand-dyed and as-is wool, trapunto, and beading on linen. Adapted from an art nouveau book by Dover Publications, Inc., and designed and hooked by Grace Collette, Chester, New Hampshire, 2017.

Grace Collette
Chester, New Hampshire

Grace is a retired accountant. She's been the secretary of White Mountain Woolen Magic for eight years and is a Maine Tin Pedlar, a Seacoast Rugger, and belongs to two local groups. This is her seventh appearance in Celebration.

The Blessed Virgin

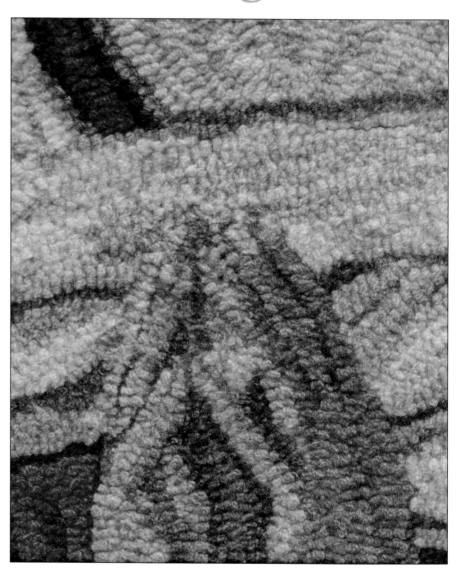

This piece is a faithful rendition of a Giovanni Battista Salvi da Sassoferrato painting of the Virgin Mary created in the 1600s. Sassoferrato is said to have influenced the famous artist Raphael.

I really learned tweaking when working on this rug. For me, getting the small, angelic smile and her hands in prayer were the parts I worked the hardest on. I found that I had to get her fingers in and then start the tweaking process of getting the definition of fingernails, knuckles, and shadows. There were many times when I had to go back and change maybe three loops of color to get the effect I wanted. The light skin tones of Mary were dyed using a dye bath from avocado pits, and the rest of the wools were from my stash. The piece was created with Dorr flannel wools in a #3 cut.

When finishing the rug, I wanted a frame that would create a look as if the piece had been hung in a room in an estate for centuries, filling the home with a quiet presence, something that had always been there and would always remain there.

One of my dear friends, a rug hooking student herself, found that she had contracted a serious illness. For my friend, her faith is a large part of who she is and what sustains her. I felt that by creating this piece for her, she would be given a sense of peace as she moved through her illness. It was deeply personal for me to hook this because so much of my love for my friend was hooked into each loop. It taught me the importance of caring deeply about a friend and making art from the heart. Any time I can hook from the heart, I learn a lot about myself and who I want to be.

Liz Marino
South Egremont, Massachusetts

Liz is the executive director of Canine Link Therapy Dogs. She's also a rug-hooking teacher and llama farmer. She is a member of several guilds and has been awarded the Sauder Village People's Choice, Sauder Award, and Green Mountain Rug Hooking Guild Viewer's Choice. This is her sixth appearance in Celebration.

The Blessed Virgin, 14½" x 18", #3-cut wool on rug warp. Adapted from a painting by Giovanni Battista Salvi da Sassoferrato and designed and hooked by Liz Marino, South Egremont, Massachusetts, 2017. JANE MCWHORTER

The Catastrophe

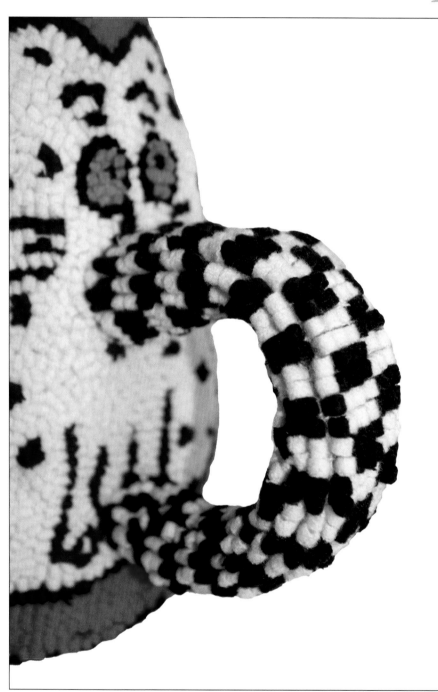

carded wool for felting the knob on the lid. The lining was gifted to me at a quilt vending event. I loved the brightness of the material and how the red, white, and black repeated the colors of the teapot.

I wanted high contrast and vibrant color to complement the funky pattern. I used black and white washed Dorr wool, a found piece of old skirting in a blue-purple, and dyed the red and green in a simple dye bath method on the stove.

I particularly like the checkerboard black and white handle against the white of the cats and the bright red. I also enjoy the Rastafarian teapot hat (lid) and the goofy cat grins, and how each cat has a different personality.

The teapot was hand-sewn together using upholstery thread and the ladder stitch. The inner cotton lining was assembled on a sewing machine and then again hand-basted to the teapot. The teapot lid was padded slightly with carded wool before the lining was hand-sewn on to give the lid more structure and help it stay in place.

Conceptualizing a flat design into the round is challenging. A paper template would have been useful and provided an idea of where the spout and handle would appear in relation to the cats. Perhaps you can guess how the name of the piece came about. I had a serious "Yikes!" moment after sewing the spout and handle in place!

I love the breadth of rug hooking; one can work on a piece either in miniature or 8' x 10' or bigger, in either a #2 cut or with hand-torn strips, or create realistic representational images or primitive or traditional designs. The scope seems endless, and the color and dyeing are forever fascinating and wonderful. Best of all, one can rug hook almost anywhere, and either all day long or in twenty-minute increments, as time allows.

I have been having fun with various 3-D objects for a few years. Last fall, I took a three-dimensional rug hooking class with Holly Kingdon that presented shaped objects that we then "decorated."

One of the shapes I worked on was the teapot. The shape was created by Holly, but the cat design was my own.

Most of the materials are wool: wool strips, wool yarn for whipping, and

The Catastrophe, 16" x 11", #4- and 5-cut hand-dyed and as-is wool on linen. 3-D teapot shape designed by Holly Kingdon, artwork designed and hooked by Lynne Howard, Calgary, Alberta, Canada, 2017. TRACY FEWSTER

Lynne Howard
Calgary, Alberta, Canada

Lynne recently retired from working as an information analyst describing information on the Canadian Arctic. She belongs to the Chinook Guild of Fibre Arts, Calgary; ATHA; and the National Guild of Pearl K. McGown Hookrafters. This is her fourth appearance in Celebration.

The Observer

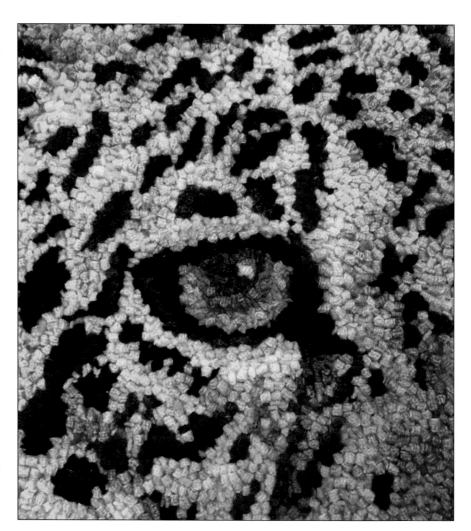

I began this rug for a class with Elizabeth Black at the Green Mountain Rug School in 1993. Big cats have always been fascinating to me, and when I saw the photograph of this jaguar, I knew I had found my subject. This wall hanging was designed using Frans Lanting's photograph as inspiration.

The colors of the jaguar were dictated by his natural coloration, but the colors of the foliage were dyed not only to complement him but also to set him off and provide the perfect foil.

The background was particularly challenging and is the reason I put this away for twenty-five years. Drawing the foliage was difficult—how much is enough without being too much? How much negative space does the jaguar need around it? When I worked on this twenty-five years ago, I tried numerous ways of completing the background, but none felt right. In July 2017, I was selected for an artist residency at the Kingsbrae International Residence for the Arts in New Brunswick, Canada. Working in my own studio there, surrounded by natural beauty and given the time just to design and hook, the background began to emerge. Suddenly I could envision it all. Foreground, middle ground, and background fell into place. I redrew the foliage and dabbled with dye to create the dense jungle with the very subtle leaves. My final pieces of wool looked strangely like camouflage.

With this rug, I learned that sometimes your original vision cannot be completed. Time and distance change your point of view and skill, as they should. Picking up an old unfinished piece again allows you to look at it with fresh eyes and listen to the song you are composing together. The piece will have a voice, but you must listen.

As a young bride in Halifax, Nova Scotia, in 1976, we needed rugs to cover our floors. I saw a semicircular rug with a bowl of fruit on the cover of *Woman's Day Magazine* and thought I'd found just the thing. I could hook my own rugs! Rug hooking has helped me realize and develop artistic talent I was frequently told as a child that I didn't have. From my first moment hooking, I never looked at anything in the same way. Everything had a turn of shape, line, a nuance of color, and a texture that made my fingers tingle. Hooking on a daily basis smooths out my life and helps me gain perspective. It is my yoga.

In The Judges' Eyes: *The body is worked behind the grasses very well. Values bring the subject out of the darkness; Well executed. The eyes and the snout are good. The animal is the main subject, and the green leaves and background add to the piece but do not take over.*

The Observer, 21" x 23½", #3- to 5-cut hand-dyed wool on linen. Adapted with permission from a photograph by Frans Lanting/lanting.com and designed and hooked by Cheryl G.W. Orcutt, Peterborough, New Hampshire, 2017.

Cheryl G.W. Orcutt
Peterborough, New Hampshire

Cheryl is a special education teacher and reading specialist. She belongs to the Green Mountain Rug Hooking Guild. She was a founding member of the White Mountain Woolen Magic Guild and is the incoming vice president. This is her second appearance in Celebration.

The Origin of Inspiration

This rug was a close adaptation of a painting by artist Carrie Martinez, of Gainesville, Florida, who kindly gave me permission in March 2017 to hook it as a rug. I had been wanting to hook a rug with a peacock for some time and was looking for unusual ideas. I came across this piece of artwork shortly after having viewed a traveling exhibit of the hooked tarot in New Jersey in February 2017. I was so impressed by that rug exhibit. A lot of Carrie Martinez's beautiful artwork is mainly in the mystical, surreal, tarot-esque realm, so this piece really spoke to me. Plus, it gave me the opportunity to hook a peacock for the first time. I'm grateful to Carrie Martinez for allowing me to hook her lovely *Origin of Inspiration*.

When creating this piece, I was trying to stay close to the colors of the original artwork. I dyed all the wool myself, using a variety of straight dyeing, spot dyeing, and overdyeing, except for a very small amount of as-is wool that I incorporated with my hand-dyed wool within the highly variegated green in the forest edge. The forest edging was actually the most difficult to hook, as it was a visually complicated part of the design. Even though it was a small part of the rug, it took the longest to finish. I really just had to tackle that part very slowly and deliberately, closely studying the original artwork as I hooked that area.

With this rug, I learned that, for me, it's quite a challenge to closely imitate a rather intricate piece of painted artwork in wool. In other adaptations that I have hooked, I've adjusted design and/or color to suit my own tastes or to more easily translate to hooking. This rug stretched me in both my hooking abilities, and my dyeing abilities since I wanted the design and the colors to be very close to the artist's painting.

My mother-in-law, Marjorie Gilbert Anderson, a McGown Certified Instructor, taught me to hook in 1987. However, I only completed one simple piece then and had to set it aside as a hobby, since career and family were consuming my time. She encouraged me to reconnect with hooking when I retired, and I began hooking again in 2015. I love all the creative aspects of rug hooking, from design to dyeing wool to pulling loops. I am just over three years into hooking and keep challenging myself to expand in all areas of hooking. I find great joy and inspiration in seeing work done by other rug hookers, as there is always something to learn.

In The Judges' Eyes: *The deco style is interpreted with pure colors and long lines of hooking; Interesting elements like the peacock tail and border of trees keep you looking; Nice all around rug. Pretty color plan. Nice job on the peacock.*

Jane Anderson
Clinton, New Jersey

Jane is a retired marketing director at Alcatel-Lucent. She is currently secretary of the Hunterdon County Rug Artisans Guild (HCRAG) in New Jersey and is a member of ATHA. This is her second appearance in Celebration.

The Origin of Inspiration, 19¼" x 35½", #2- to 6-cut hand-dyed and as-is wool and yarn on linen. Adapted with permission from artwork by Carrie Martinez and designed and hooked by Jane Anderson, Clinton, New Jersey, 2017.

Tiger Close Up

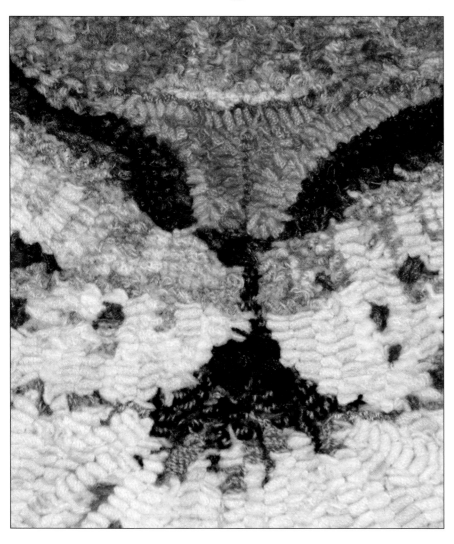

animal. Seeing the eyes come to life and look back at me from the end of my hook is what keeps me hooking animals. The most challenging part was the very large nose. It's basically one color (no stripes), but it was important that it didn't look flat. By keeping the center of the nose lighter than the sides, I was able to obtain a rounded look. I used many as-is textured wools to create the realistic look of fur. I love to mix wools to obtain the subtle color and value changes I see in my visual aids. Textures allow you to create magic, particularly with animals.

To finish the rug, I zigzagged the edges, turned the monk's cloth toward the back over cording, basted it in place, and then whipped the edges with wool yarn. I also used rug tape, and I attached one side while I was whipping the edges. Then I hand-sewed the other edge of the tape to the back.

This rug was another lesson in "thinking big." I normally use a #4 cut and hook smaller pieces. Using a #8 cut, and then translating what I saw in my visual aid to a much larger area, was a challenge. With a wide cut, you cover more area when hooking, but it also takes longer to see if you are obtaining the realistic details you want to achieve.

I first started rug hooking after I took a beginner class with Pat Moyer in 1993, and I've been hooked ever since. Rug hooking challenges me and allows me to express my creativity. I also find rug hooking to be soothing and restful. The repetitive movements help to relax me and clear my mind.

*T*iger Close Up is the second in a series of wide-cut (#8), close-up animal rugs. The pattern is adapted from a photo by Lunasa Photography of a tiger, which is at T&D's Cats of the World in Penns Creek, Pennsylvania, which I visit every year. The beautiful photo spoke to me, and I knew it would be a great companion piece to my wide-cut *Cougar Close Up*.

I am always drawn to the eyes. They speak to me first, then I see the rest of the

Judy Carter
Willow Street, Pennsylvania

Judy is a bank branch manager, a master artisan with the PA Guild of Craftsmen, and the author of Hooking Animals. *She's a member of the Woolwrights and Hunterdon County Rug Artisans Guilds of ATHA and the Conestoga Chapter of McGown. This is her fourteenth appearance in* Celebration.

Tiger Close Up, 20" x 26", #4-, 6- & 8-cut hand-dyed and as-is wool on monk's cloth. Adapted with permission from a photo by Lunasa Photography and designed and hooked by Judy Carter, Willow Street, Pennsylvania, 2017.

Van Gogh Self Portrait 1887

I love Impressionist artwork. There are many fabulous impressionist painters, but Van Gogh has always been one of my favorites. I have seen his *Starry Night*, *Wheat Field with Cypresses*, and *Sunflowers* hooked into rugs but had not seen a self-portrait done. And after reading *Lust for Life* by Irving Stone, I knew it was a challenge I wanted to take on.

To get the look I wanted, I gathered many of my scrap wool pieces. I didn't keep track, but I'm sure there are hundreds of different shades of color in this rug. I did end up dyeing a few values, especially for the teal, which was an important part of the overall rug. This self-portrait is all about color variety, but I'm constantly learning more about value, and I felt like I really learned a lot from this rug about how powerful value is when hooking. I'm starting to see that value is more flexible than color, and that can be fun and freeing when you are hooking.

I enjoyed hooking the nose and mouth best and was most pleased with the results there. Again, I loved seeing how the value of the color (and not the actual color) determined the shape of the nose and mouth. As usual for me, the most challenging part

of this rug was his eyes. I struggle with hooking eyes, whether for people or animals. I kind of feel they are the pathway to the soul, so it's important to try and get them right. Because Van Gogh led somewhat of a tortured life, I wanted his eyes to reflect a bit of that sadness.

About twelve years ago, I took a beginner rug hooking class with Gail Dufresne. Since the class was in my hometown of Clinton, New Jersey, and I had always wanted to learn how to hook traditional rugs, I jumped at the chance. I was additionally blessed to find out that Gail had a studio in a nearby town. So that was it; I was hooked! Since that time, I have been blessed to be able to benefit from many teachers. I also enjoy the deep friendships I have made over the years. What a wonderful community of people! Rug hooking provides all the elements I crave from a creative pursuit. The design principles and choices, the options of colors and values, the techniques with dyeing, and the satisfaction of completing a piece of art from beginning to end are all parts of the joy I get from rug hooking.

Therese Shick
Annandale, New Jersey

Therese is a mother and belongs to the Hunterdon County Rug Artisans Guild, Alice Beatty and Yankees Chapters of ATHA, and the Brandywine Rug Hooking Guild. This is her second appearance in Celebration.

Van Gogh Self Portrait 1887 , 28" x 33", #3- to 5-cut as-is and overdyed wool on linen. Adapted from a painting by Vincent Van Gogh and designed and hooked by Therese Shick, Annandale, New Jersey, 2017.
MAUREEN NOWAK

Wilson's on the Lake

I had saved this picture from a calendar several years ago. I loved the beautiful fall picture of a country store with a "woody" parked outside. Since it did not have the name of the artist on it, I went to. . . yes, Google. . . and found the image. I contacted George Kovach, the artist, and requested permission to hook an adaptation of his painting. He granted it and enjoyed seeing the finished rug.

I tried to duplicate all the beautiful and rich fall colors of the original painting. I used only leftover, mostly dip-dyed, wool from previous rugs for *Wilson's on the Lake*. I particularly loved hooking the old car! It was fun to think about cars from long ago and how they have changed. This was also the first rug I've hooked that dealt with so many shadows, especially on the roof. It was interesting to see how a mauve color brought out those shadows. I learned that shadows can be extremely important in capturing a certain feel of a painting or rug. The shadows in this rug made it feel like a beautiful fall afternoon at a country store by the lake.

The detail in this rug was the most challenging aspect. As I have done in previous detailed rugs, I used the method to hooking details described by Eric Sandberg in *Rug Hooking* magazine

(*Le Chateau Rug*). I turn my rug upside down while hooking the details. I find that when I'm doing that, I'm not concentrating on getting the exact image hooked but getting the position of the colors right. Once right side up, the image magically appears.

I started rug hooking in 2003 when I retired and moved to North Carolina. A woman I had worked with encouraged me to give rug hooking a try. To date, I have completed more than 150 hooked pieces, including a room-sized rug. Like reading a good book, rug hooking takes you to beautiful places. It allows you to explore your own creativity and share ideas with other fiber artists. It relaxes me, gives me a sense of accomplishment, and provides me with a greater appreciation for color!

In The Judges' Eyes: *Love the shadows on that white building and decision to wash out the sky so we look at the cooler blue shadows and interesting details; Executed with knowledge of an artist and what it takes to rug hook a pictorial—congratulations!; The car is especially fine.*

Wilson's on the Lake, 29" x 22", #3- to 6-cut wool on rug warp. Adapted with permission from a painting by George Kovach and designed and hooked by Karen Whidden, Southern Pines, North Carolina, 2017. JOHN WHIDDEN

Karen Whidden
Southern Pines, North Carolina

Karen is a retired director of customer service for water, gas, and electric utilities. She belongs to a group of local fiber artists who meet twice a month at the Senior Enrichment Center in Pinehurst, North Carolina. This is her tenth appearance in Celebration.

Woman on Horse in Mountains

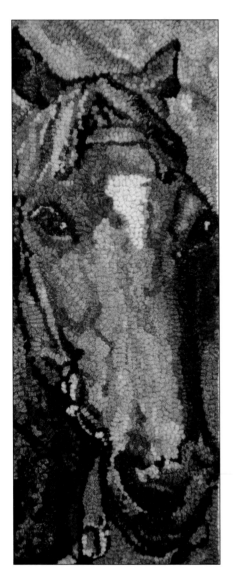

Woman on Horse in Mountains, a painting by William H.D. Koerner (1878–1938), graced the October 6, 1928 cover of *The Saturday Evening Post*. Although I discovered the cover nearly ninety years after its initial creation, it spoke to me with a modern relevance. I felt that Koerner captured the serenity and beauty of the landscape, horse, and rider as he conveyed the strong, independent spirit of the woman and the sense of adventure of the moment.

The moment I saw *The Saturday Evening Post* cover, I thought of my mother—born in 1928 and raised on a working ranch nestled in the mountains—because she exemplifies all of the qualities that Koerner's illustration called to my mind. I immediately wanted to paint it with wool as a gift to her. I hoped to show her how much I appreciate her independent spirit and love of horses and the outdoors—especially the mountains—and to thank her for her efforts to pass these traits on to me and my daughters. Mom loves the rug and says it reflects the best aspects of ranch life that a young woman could experience, then and now.

This rug came to life under the tutelage of Diane Stoffel, an extraordinarily talented and patient teacher. As Diane guided me through this project, she was generous with her knowledge and encouragement. Using her artist's eye, Diane helped me to understand Koerner's style and to appreciate how he balanced bold swaths of vibrant color with delicate details to create depth and mood. One of the most important concepts Diane taught me is that every loop is an audition for the final work, and it is only at the end of the project that the final determination is made whether it will become part of the final production.

In 2010, I spotted a hand-hooked rug in one of the booths at the Maryland Sheep & Wool Festival. I left there with a pattern, a hook, a bag full of woolen worms, and a new obsession. It was love at first loop. I contacted an artist who hooked many of my favorite rugs to inquire if she would teach me about the art form and her style of hooking. That talented artist, Ann Winterling, graciously answered my email and generously offered to help me learn. Ann taught me that in order to be the kind of hooker I wanted to be, I would need to develop an artist's eye, and that I should sketch and study and never give up. She proved to be a terrific mentor, and I am grateful she introduced me to the side of hooking that impacts the project long before the first loop is pulled.

Nancy Samuels
La Cañada Flintridge, California

Nancy is a lawyer. She comes from a family of artists. Her father teaches upholstery, her grandmothers were both seamstresses and knitters, and her great-grandmother tatted. Nancy also sews, quilts, knits, and crochets. This is her first appearance in Celebration.

Woman on Horse in Mountains, 22" x 29", #3- to 5-cut hand-dyed and as-is wool on monk's cloth. Adapted from artwork by William H.D. Koerner and designed and hooked by Nancy Samuels, La Cañada Flintridge, California, 2017. MARY WORTMAN

Borders

The idea for this rug first popped into my mind because I wanted a fresh look for our back hall. It had two of the first rugs I ever made on the floor, and they were looking kind of tired since they were forty years old. I had made a table runner eight years ago that featured different borders, so I thought if I expanded that idea to a long hall runner, it would work well. The hall runner uses the same colors as the table runner (gold, red, and green), but they are placed differently for the floor runner.

Red, gold, and green are some of my favorite colors, and I love the combination of them together. I added the antique paisley because of the texture; it helped tie the other colors together. Since the runner is so long, I used a lot of textures to add visual interest.

The three borders that are 3-D geometric (the two end borders and one near the middle) were the most challenging sections. The borders had a very 3-D look, so it was tricky to get the values right. I had to do a bit of ripping out before I found the right combination.

This sounds silly, but I had forgotten just how much wool a big rug takes. I would think I had plenty of one color, only to find I needed more. Thankfully, because each border is a separate design element, if the colors were a bit different, it did not matter. A good example is the golds I used. There are actually many different pieces of gold used. In the end, I think this gives the rug more interest. Although the rug was designed for our back hall, it turned

out so well, my husband and I decided it had to have a more prominent place. It now resides in our master bedroom's bathroom. We get to see it all the time, which is really nice!

I first got started in rug hooking after seeing an article in a magazine. I taught myself how to hook (with *no* frame at first). I made a few rugs in the next couple of years and then became interested in other fiber arts. Then, twenty years later, we moved to our current home, and I met other rug hookers. I started hooking again and haven't stopped since. I enjoy rug hooking because of the beauty that can be created and the meditative quality of pulling up hoops. I also love the creative process of designing my own patterns.

Lyle Drier
Waukesha, Wisconsin

Lyle is retired from owning her own antique business. Her rugs have won a number of ribbons at the Wisconsin State Fair, Sauder Village, and LeDuc Museum. They've also been shown at numerous hook-ins, the Museum of Wisconsin Artists, and the Wisconsin Museum of Quilts & Fiber Art. This is her thirteenth appearance in Celebration.

Borders, 28" x 96", #4- to 6-cut hand-dyed, spot-dyed, as-is, and antique paisley wool on monk's cloth. Designed and hooked by Lyle Drier, Waukesha, Wisconsin, 2016. DENNIS DRIER

In The Judges' Eyes: *Bold and exciting palette; Great variety in the various bands and motifs of the runner, but the careful use of color keeps it from being jarring; Outstanding design, color, and detail. All around great rug.*

Posy Sheep

I started this rug at the Woolly Fox Rug Camp in Ligonier, Pennsylvania in 2016 with my teacher, Janice Johnson. Her beautiful wool and advice helped me create a rug that I really love. I own fiber animals as pets (sheep, goats, and alpacas), so I am drawn to designs with sheep. I loved the idea of using lots of neutral colors. I wanted to play with layers of dark and light textures but also wanted to add a touch of soft color in the flowers. After camp was over, I became busy with other obligations, and the rug sat unfinished for a year. I finally convinced myself that I should take the rug out of the bag and finish the hooking. I felt a little overwhelmed at first because even though I had hooked the center motif at camp, there were still so many more design elements to hook! I had a general idea of what I wanted the finished rug to look like, but sometimes I ended up making last-minute color choices while I was hooking.

While I liked the sheep, of course, my favorite part to hook turned out to be the funky branch shapes that run around the outside border. I mixed two brown and cream nubby textures together and filled the "vein" of the branch with an old red plaid. I liked the contrast that it created. I also liked mixing many of the lighter textures to form the variety of "tabs" along the branches.

There were so many layers to this design. When I started hooking it, I

felt a little overwhelmed and lost with what I wanted to do. I hooked the center portion with the sheep and then moved on to the next layer, which was the flowers, then hooked the outer border last. I tried not to think too far ahead, and this helped me to keep my focus for what I wanted to accomplish.

I am a self-taught rug hooker. After seeing stacks and stacks of hand-dyed wool stored on a large shelving rack, I decided to explore the art of rug hooking. I wanted to find out how all those luscious colors were used in a rug! Rug hooking is relaxing and portable, and I love using textures and soft colors. I love to see how a design unfolds as I am hooking it.

Kris Miller
Howell, Michigan

Kris owns a rug hooking business (Spruce Ridge Studios) and is a pattern designer and rug hooking teacher. She is also the author of Introduction to Rug Hooking. *She's won ribbons at her county fair and state fair and was included several times as an artisan in the* Early American Life Directory *for Traditional American Crafts.* This is her fourth appearance in Celebration.

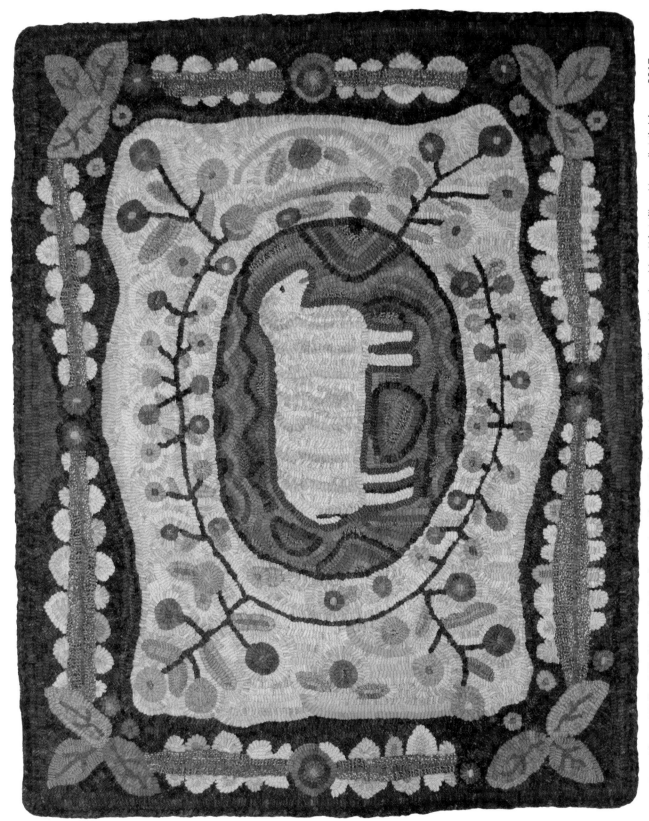

Posy Sheep. 22½" x 30", #8- and 8.5-cut wool on linen. Designed by Sally Kallin and hooked by Kris Miller, Howell, Michigan, 2017.

A Bunny for Margaret, 28" x 41½", #4- to 6-cut hand-dyed and as-is wool on linen. Adapted with permission from a painting by Anna King and designed and hooked by Jan King, Mt. Pleasant, South Carolina, 2017. ANNA KING

Outside the Box, 49" x 67", #5-, 6- and 8-cut hand-dyed and textured wool on linen. Adapted with permission from a quilt pattern by Jessica J.E. Smith and hooked by Susan Grant, Georgetown, Ontario, Canada, 2016. FISHBACK PHOTOGRAPHY

Tangled Trot, 54" x 36", #3- to 8-cut hand-dyed, recycled, and as-is wool on linen. Designed and hooked by Nancy Qualls, Hooksett, New Hampshire, 2017.

Steam Punk Tangle, 28" x 23", #6-cut hand-dyed and as-is wool on linen. Designed and hooked by Laurie Wiles, Edmonton, Alberta, Canada, 2017. MELANIE COUCHER

Capitol Plaza Hotel
Montpelier, Vermont
JUNE 22-29, 2019

Teachers to Include:
Stephanie Allen-Krauss
Liz Alpert Fay
Ellen Banker
Capri Boyle Jones
Davey DeGraff
Susan Feller
Lucille Festa
Pam Kirk
Mariah Krauss
Rachelle LeBlanc
Michele Micarelli
Lisanne Miller
Bob Privé

GREEN MOUNTAIN RUG SCHOOL
www.GreenMountainHookedRugs.com

West County Bounty, 36" x 48", #4- to 6-cut hand-dyed wool on linen. Designed and hooked by Brigitta Phy, Sebastopol, California, 2017. BRUCE SHIPPEE

Brushes, 19" x 22", #5- and 6-cut hand-dyed wool on monk's cloth. Adapted from a painting by Joshua Kislevitz, designed by Norma Batastini, and hooked by Nara De Alcantara, River Edge, New Jersey, 2017. ISA AYDIN

Owl Over the Cottage, 27½" x 40½", wool yarn on rug warp. Designed and hooked by Fumiyo Heinig, Burlington, Ontario, Canada, 2017. CHRIS HAYHURST

Winter Games, 33" x 23½", Mostly #8-cut wool with some white wool yarn on linen. Designed and hooked by Carolyn Godfread, Bismarck, North Dakota, 2017.

Claire's Hen Party, 42" x 28", #8- and 9-cut hand-dyed and as-is wool on linen. Designed by Jane McGown Flynn and hooked by Patsy Gorveatte, Black Point, Nova Scotia, Canada, 2017.

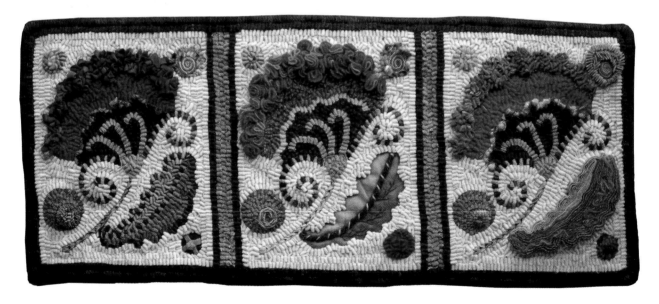

Three Flowers, 26½" x 10¾", #4- to 8-cut hand-dyed and as-is wool, silk, velvet, roving, hand-dyed and specialty yarns, grosgrain ribbon, needle-felted wool, and embroidery floss on linen. Designed by Bea Brock and hooked by Helen Mar Parkin, Lindale, Texas, 2016.

Ad Index